"As a clinical psychologist working in the addiction field, I se
tools for my clients to avoid relapse. *Mind-Body Workbook for*
sionals have been waiting for. It explains relapse as the complex behavior it is, and a
liant explanations and exercises to not only understand cravings, but also combat them. It is my hope that
this book becomes part of every treatment center's approach to preparing their clients for lifelong sobriety."

—**Adam Gorman, PsyD**, clinical psychologist, Albany, NY

"There is genius in this book. My reaction after reading it was I wanted to stand up and cheer. This is
practical, brilliantly taught mindfulness brought to the service of relapse prevention. It is also a beautifully
transcendent document. I hope this book has a huge readership and usage because it's going to save lives."

—**John Dupuy, MA**, author of *Integral Recovery*

"*Mind-Body Workbook for Addiction* takes the mystery out of treating addiction by providing a blueprint
for connecting thoughts, feelings, behavior, and change. I plan to use this in my addiction counseling
practice."

—**Patrick McKiernan PhD**, clinical director of Certified Counseling Services, Louisville, KY

"The gap in addiction treatment that has caused so many to relapse has been finally closed! *Mind-Body
Workbook for Addiction* supplies the reader with easy-to-apply, everyday tools that allow them to access
and utilize their own innate wellspring of healing, goodness, and wisdom to live their best clean and
sober lives."

—**Peter D. Farr, MD, DABFM**, medical director of addiction medicine at Dearborn County
Hospital in Lawrenceburg, IN, and member of the American Society of Addiction Medicine

"Ongoing advances in neuroscience now confirm undeniably that addiction involves the neural activity
of the brain as much as the physiology of the body and the emotional state of the inner life. *Mind-Body
Workbook for Addiction* integrates each of these into an accessible and highly effective tool for recovery,
one that will be useful for a lifetime. Every day, over five hundred people die from addiction. This is a
book that may save your life."

—**Davelyn V. Vidrine, PhD, LCSW**, director of education at the Wayne Institute for Advanced
Psychotherapy at Bellarmine University, Louisville, KY

MIND-BODY
WORKBOOK
for addiction

Effective Tools for
Substance-Abuse Recovery
& Relapse Prevention

STANLEY H. BLOCK, MD
CAROLYN BRYANT BLOCK
& GUY DU PLESSIS, MA
with RICH LANDWARD, LCSW

NEW HARBINGER PUBLICATIONS, INC.

Publisher's Note

The information contained in this workbook is intended to be educational. The authors and publisher are in no way liable for any use or misuse of the information. The ideas, techniques, and suggestions in this workbook are not intended as a substitute for expert medical, substance abuse, or mental health diagnosis, advice, or treatment. If you are under the care of health care professionals, please consult with them before altering your treatment plan. All names and identifying information of individuals in this workbook have been disguised to protect their anonymity.

Distributed in Canada by Raincoast Books

Copyright © 2016 by Stanley H. Block and Carolyn Bryant Block
      New Harbinger Publications, Inc.
      5674 Shattuck Avenue
      Oakland, CA 94609
      www.newharbinger.com

Printed in the United States of America

Acquired by Jess O'Brien; Cover design by Amy Shoup; Edited by Melanie Bell

Library of Congress Cataloging-in-Publication Data on file

Printed in the United States of America

20   19   18

10 9 8 7 6 5 4 3

CONTENTS

Foreword   V

Introduction   1

1   Come to Your Senses and Overcome Cravings   5

2   Deal Effectively with High-Risk Situations   21

3   Manage Negative Thinking and Heal Toxic Shame   41

4   Why Your Best Efforts Seem to Go Wrong   61

5   Learn How to Turn Off Your Addiction Switch   87

6   Build Healthy Relationships   105

7   Take Charge of Your Emotions   133

8   Achieve Lasting Recovery and Live Your Best Life   155

    Appendix A: Mind-Body Bridging Daily Mapping Guide   189

    Appendix B: Mind-Body Language   193

    References   197

    Acknowledgments   199

FOREWORD

What would you think if I promised you a practical approach to addiction and recovery that would yield immediately observable results? In the spate of new books every year on recovery, how many really have something new, much less something profound, to offer?

This book you are holding is a guide to changing your life at its very roots. This, by the way, is the definition of the word "radical": to the *root* or heart of the matter! So it is that you're perched now, as reader and applier-of-reading, on the very precipice of a radically game-changing paradigm shift in your life.

Philosopher of science Thomas Kuhn, who coined both the terms "paradigm" and "paradigm shift" in modern usage, offered as a memorable example the monumental shift that occurred when Copernicus had the audacity to maintain scientifically that the earth was not the center of the universe (which his contemporaries proclaimed to be the utmost of heresies).

Kuhn speaks to the breakdown of any scientific model, or paradigm, as resulting from a gradual accumulation of internal and external problems, or "anomalies." At a certain point, the weight of so many exceptions and anomalies to common or scientific sense breaks the back of the former system, making way for something new to arise. Copernicus's genius (and courage) was to proffer a brand-new model of the entire universe, one which not only synced up with the way things really are, but also formed the basis for so many of the advances of modernity.

This is not a book on astronomy or physics, but it is no less paradigm-shifting in its intent and its expression. The authors are fully aware of the landscape into which they write. They intend to challenge old ways of thinking which do not work, and propose new ways which both personal experience and empirical research support as indeed being highly effective...and life-saving.

Mind-body bridging, or MBB for short, which lies at the very center of this model of recovery, is indeed an approach to addiction that has already proven highly effective in the treatment of substance abuse (right through research published in professional journals in 2015!). Plain and simple, MBB teaches mindful awareness skills combined with cognitive and behavioral strategies, with a twist (more to follow). And it works!

What you have with MBB is a prescription for a *new/old* approach to recovery that simply must be incorporated into substance abuse studies and treatment, if the field of addiction recovery is to progress radically enough to save lives that are otherwise being tragically lost. (By "new/old" I only mean to indicate that this bold book draws upon the best of previous and crucial groundwork in the field, such as the 12-step process, as well as incorporating and innovating upon the very most current breakthroughs in brain science and addiction.)

What, pray tell, do I mean by the previous statement: "If the field of addiction recovery is to progress radically enough to save lives that are otherwise being tragically lost"? Having worked for decades now in this field, including at nationally known rehab treatment centers and with clients from every stratum of society and economics, I can definitively assert that clients who leave rehabs (after a good and decent start) relapse and die in droves, oftentimes within months of moving back into their lives post–acute treatment. *This is not working!*

While I am not so naïve as to suggest that there is only one issue at stake here—there are in fact many—I do know that rhetoric alone, even about psychological tools for addressing trauma or the essential role of spiritual resources, is simply insufficient in the face of addiction and post–acute withdrawal syndrome (PAWS). To address what is truly at stake here, the authors describe in extraordinarily concise and clear ways two opposing brain systems: the *default-mode network* and the *executive network*. Understood most simply, the default-mode network, when activated, hijacks the addict's or recovering addict's natural sense of well-being and resourcefulness, especially in the face of external or internal triggers. The latter system, the executive network, is most often trumped by the default mode; and without intervention, relapse is nearly guaranteed. There's more…

In elucidating that "more," the authors use what philosophers call "Occam's razor," by cutting through all the overwhelming complexities inherent in microanalytic science, and offering up a practically useful condensation of the last decade of post–brain scan research (never possible before, because the necessary technology did not yet exist). When the authors here explain brain systems which either impede or facilitate sturdy recovery, you the reader leave with a highly accurate model of what's going on with your central nervous system in and around addiction recovery. More importantly, you are given a pathway that, as applied to your individual existence, will change your brain and your life. It's that radical…and that simple!

If relapse for those in recovery is preceded by overpowering craving (drug-wanting), then what coping skills do you, as a recovering addict, need most to withstand the magnetic power of those cravings? The authors aim right to the core of this question, and they provide a carefully detailed, immediately applicable approach to relaxing the activated default-mode brain network (see above) and restoring in its place the executive network, which is the basis of our resilience, sense of balance, and successful relapse prevention.

Now the true litmus test here—whether this book makes a difference or not—lies completely in your own hands. Let me tell you a story: When I first met the co-authors by Skype, Dr. Block asked me if I would be willing to try an exercise (straight out of this book). Now mind you: he didn't start pontificating, or even instructing me, about this book. Rather, he invited me into an experience. Having nothing to lose, I of course volunteered to follow. The exercise, quite elementary in form, had quick and palpable results in my own awareness. These changes then became the foundation for our subsequent dialogue into what the model is, and what it intends to accomplish. Notice again: experience first, commentary only later.

That day, Dr. Block helped me to access the most essential part of me, what he calls "the inner wellspring of healing, goodness, and wisdom," which itself may be correlated with the above executive brain system. Once accessed, my distress and imbalance, engendered by the default-mode network, soon and quite literally evaporated. Of course, it took my agreeing to practice his simple exercise. (And this book is chock full of them, trust me!)

Well, it is that same spirit—of personally investing, as I did with Dr. Block, in a process of gradual transformation—that you must bring to this volume. I myself know, now, that the authors aspire to nothing less than changing the world for the positive with this MBB model being implemented writ large—whether in individual lives (yours and mine) or in larger organizational and even political applications. So here you have true pioneers, with their proposed MBB model of recovery treatment—one might rightly say, an MBB *model of life*. Their model, MBB, lays out practical guidelines complementary to the very best of the time-tested wisdom of the 12-step traditions, even while extending them powerfully and without apology. Their model, MBB, likewise complements the best of all major psychological/therapeutic methods and models (from cognitive-behavioral to humanistic/existential to psychoanalytic), while convincingly critiquing each of them for common, sometimes hamstringing, limitations.

Their core objection, and corrective, to most psychological and spiritually based models of addressing addiction lies in this central insight: you don't need to fix that which isn't broken. Or to use a common-sense visual, you don't need to reinvent the sun to receive its life-giving rays. Rather, remove the clouds which may at times obscure the sun, and all shall be well! Back to the book: all that our bodies and brains need for recovery, whether from addiction or the countless other afflictions of existence, is restoration of our innate orientation toward our "sun": what Block calls "the inner wellspring of healing, goodness, and wisdom." Uncover and remove that which may interfere (a stressed-out default brain mode), and voila, recovery (to the executive brain) is as natural a response as is the baby's first breath upon delivery into its new world.

When I started here by introducing Kuhn on paradigm shifts, I wasn't attempting to be literary. This book is a paradigm shift in recovery work, in spiritual discourse, in contemporary psychological theory and practice, and of most importance, *in your own life*. Read this book...apply it to your day-to-day existence...and prepare yourself for the mother of all paradigm shifts!

—Robert Weathers, PhD
California Southern University
Irvine, California
July 4, 2015

INTRODUCTION

Nobody knows how difficult it is for you to stop using drugs. You keep on relapsing even though you have made commitments to yourself and loved ones to stop. There are times when it seems as though your body and mind have been hijacked by such an uncontrollable urge to use that you simply give in to it. You feel like you are walking around with a *relapse time bomb* that can be triggered at any time. You have probably tried to make changes in your life in an attempt to avoid situations or people that may trigger your relapse time bomb—most likely without much success. No wonder you are feeling frustrated and helpless.

No matter who you are and what you have been through, this mind-body workbook offers an entirely new understanding and treatment of your addiction. Within the first ten minutes of doing the exercises in this workbook, you will begin to experience and use the straightforward, easy-to-use relapse prevention and recovery tools that heal your addiction. When these tools are utilized in your everyday life, your relapse time bomb is defused, and you can live the life you were meant to live.

WHY CAN'T YOU STOP USING DRUGS?

Why is it that at certain times you are able to stay clean, and then at other times you are utterly powerless to stop a relapse? What is it that happens to you when you relapse? It's like a switch turns on inside you. Whenever that switch is on, you become powerless and do the same thing over and over again. It's as if your mind and body go on automatic pilot.

When you think back, each relapse was accompanied by a commanding mental and physical state composed of a combination of overwhelming cravings, obsessive thoughts, and a trance-like alteration of consciousness. This mind-body state is further characterized by such a profound alteration and befuddling of awareness that all you can think about is using, and the short-term pleasure or relief associated with it. In this mind-body state, full consideration of past damages or future consequences is not easily accessible. In that state, contrary to your intentions, using seems like a perfectly good and rational idea.

The foundation of the *Mind-Body Workbook for Addiction* is that this mind-body state which drives your habitual substance abuse is the result of the overactivity of a system in your mind and body called the *Identity System* (I-System). The I-System is either active (on) or at rest (off). Fortunately your I-System can be switched off with a technique known as *mind-body bridging*. When your I-System is switched off, you are able to connect with your innate source of power and wisdom. You are no longer powerless over your substance abuse, but have a choice. By utilizing the tools in this workbook you are able to manage and switch off your I-System, and naturally heal from your addiction.

THE IDENTITY SYSTEM (I-SYSTEM)

When your Identity System is active it not only affects your mind and body, but also your behavior. The I-System limits your behavior to certain predictable and habitual patterns. Your I-System has shaped a particularly limited and contracted way of life, marked by habitual substance abuse and loss of control. Therefore, your addiction is best understood as a *mode of being* (or *mode* for short), meaning that it is a particular and habitual way of existing, relating, and living. The basic premise of this workbook is that all aspects related to your *addicted mode* (thoughts, emotions, attitudes, beliefs, and behaviors), that make your life unmanageable, are the result of an overactive I-System. The I-System can drive any number of habitual modes of being, such as a depressive mode, a post-traumatic stress mode, or an anxiety mode. Previous mind-body bridging workbooks have dealt with several of these dysfunctional modes of being (Block and Block 2007; Block and Block 2010; Block and Block 2012; Block and Block 2013; Block and Block 2014). The addicted mode is also a manifestation of the I-System, which is characterized by habitual substance abuse and loss of control. For some this addicted mode progresses until it becomes one's primary way of life.

Your addiction is only in control when your I-System is active. Once the I-System is active, you live your daily life fearful of relapse, as if your mind, body, and world are your enemies. Your cravings and all other aspects of your addiction are I-System driven. Therefore, to manage and resolve your addiction, you will learn and experience how to put your I-System to rest during the activities of daily living. Through this management of your I-System, you can gain freedom from your addiction.

In this workbook you will experience that your addiction is not a permanent or chronic condition, but rather a transitory mode that is one of many possible modes of being. You are much more than just your addicted mode. This workbook focuses on the mechanism that drives your addiction, and shows you how to treat it.

WHAT IS MIND-BODY BRIDGING?

Mind-body bridging has been shown to be an effective therapeutic intervention over a wide range of medical and psychiatric conditions (Tollefson et al. 2009; Nakamura et al. 2013; Nakamura et al. 2011), including the treatment of substance abuse (Nakamura et al. 2015). Mind-body bridging is an easy way to put the I-System to rest. When your I-System is quiet, your mind and body cooperate, or bridge, to self-heal from your addiction. You are then free to live your best life.

When you are in an addicted mode your head is full of irrational urges and troubling thoughts, and your body is full of tension. In this mind and body state you experience yourself as a *damaged self*. The damaged self is not simply a mental state; it also affects every cell of your body and your entire way of being in the world. It's caused by the activity of your I-System, not by your urges, thoughts, or circumstances. This damaged self is experienced as toxic shame, which makes you feel that you are fundamentally flawed and that you need to be fixed. I-System-induced shame drives substance abuse in a futile effort to "repair" this illusion of the damaged self (Bradshaw 1988).

This workbook is based on the fact that your *mind-body* (mind and body as a unified, whole unit) can access its *natural functioning state*. This natural functioning mind-body state is your inherent *true self*, which is always functioning when your I-System is resting. When the I-System is resting, your addiction does not run your life, and you get in touch with your innate source of healing, goodness, and wisdom. This natural functioning state, the true self, is always present and can be accessed at any moment.

What sets mind-body bridging apart from other addiction treatment methods is that you are not seen as "damaged" (an illusion created by your I-System) and in need of "fixing," but rather as a complete, whole person who is always connected to a wellspring of healing, goodness, and wisdom. It is only your overactive I-System that is preventing you from experiencing and expressing this wellspring and living free from addiction. When the I-System is resting, your adaptive skills will flourish.

YOUR ADDICTION ON/OFF SWITCH

Brain research (Weissman et al. 2006; Boly et al. 2008; Cole et al. 2013) has found functionally distinct networks of the brain, including an *executive network* and a *default-mode network*. The *executive network* coordinates moment by moment how we think, feel, see the world, make decisions, and act. It's responsible for the direction and management of our lives. Conversely, when we're having exaggerated thoughts about ourselves and our experiences, the *default-mode network* is dominant, making it difficult to respond appropriately to situations as they come up.

Using fMRI (functional magnetic resonance imaging), scientists and doctors can now take pictures of how the brain changes while it is working. It has been suggested that an over-dominant default-mode network may be a sign of an active I-System and a flexibly performing executive network may be a sign of the natural functioning loop strengthened by mind-body bridging (Block, Ho, and Nakamura 2009). Brain research (Cole et al. 2013) shows that when the default-mode network is not overactive, your executive network takes charge, regulating your mind so that you function at your best. The I-System lies at the root of your addiction by putting the default-mode network on overdrive. Mind-body bridging quiets the I-System, letting you heal and function naturally in the executive mode.

Imagine a big switch in your brain that turns the I-System (overactive default-mode network) on and off. When in an addicted mode, the I-System is on and shuts down your natural functioning (executive network). The exercises in this workbook will give you the tools to "switch off" your addicted mode (over-active default-mode network). When your "addiction switch" is off, you function at your best and access your wellspring of healing, goodness, and wisdom.

MIND-BODY BRIDGING AND 12-STEP PROGRAMS

Mind-body bridging is a very powerful adjunct for those involved in working a 12-step program. Mind-body bridging and 12-step programs have a synergistic relationship; your mind-body bridging practice will be strengthened when used in conjunction with a 12-step program, and your 12-step practice will be powerfully augmented with the addition of mind-body bridging practice.

As you work through the exercises in this book, you will begin to understand and experience that what is of primary import is not only *what* you are doing, but *who* is doing it—your I-System-driven damaged self or your naturally functioning true self. Nearly all recovery programs focus on the "what" and the "how" of what you should be doing and how to do it. Mind-body bridging focuses on "who" is doing the recovery practices, your I-System-driven damaged self or your executive functioning true self. When your recovery program is driven by an active I-System it has the same goal as addiction, to "fix" the illusion of the damaged self. As with any addiction, this becomes a futile effort, because you cannot fix what is not broken. Instead of improving your well-being, this adds to your distress and feelings of inadequacy. Your recovery program can consist of healthy activities, practiced to the utmost, but if it is driven by an active I-System, it will compromise or even have a destructive effect on your well-being. In short, the addition of the principles and practices of mind-body bridging will assist individuals in working any recovery program, by adding the much-needed *who* to the *what* and the *how*.

HOW TO USE THIS BOOK

This workbook outlines the *Mind-Body Bridging Recovery (MBBR) program* that has powerful, easy-to-do exercises to heal from your addiction and build recovery resilience. In this book, you will learn a clinically validated mind-body language that allows you to know, connect with, and manage your mind and body as never before. This easy-to-understand language frames your mind-body states in terms of an active (on) or an inactive (off) I-System.

In every chapter you develop, use, and personalize the effective *recovery tools* through the simple process of *Discover, Experience,* and *Apply.* Each chapter serves as a building block for the next one. It is important to do the exercises and read each chapter in sequence, so you can create a solid foundation to move forward in healing from your addiction. As you move through the program, your list of recovery tools keeps growing, so that you can rely on them for anything that's going on in your life.

You will find an MBB (Mind-Body Bridging) Quality of Life Gauge at the beginning, middle, and end of the book. This helps you measure the changes in your life. At the end of each chapter, there is an MBB Rating Scale that lets you know how well you're using the self-healing tools you are learning. Clinical experience has shown that high scores on these rating scales are predictive of positive outcome. Therefore, the more you integrate the recovery tools in this book, the more you optimize a sustainable recovery.

For those working in the field of addiction treatment, the MBBR program outlined in the *Mind-Body Workbook for Addiction* can be presented as a cycle of eight psychoeducational groups. This workbook is best suited for those who have completed a primary care program and are motivated for recovery. It is therefore particularly suited for use in second-stage inpatient and outpatient programs, as well as aftercare programs. Additionally, this workbook is also very useful for those in later stages of recovery who want to augment their existing recovery programs. It is important to note that the MBBR program outlined in this book is not meant to replace an individual's existing recovery practices and social support system, but rather as a powerful adjunct.

CHAPTER 1

COME TO YOUR SENSES AND OVERCOME CRAVINGS

Discover, Experience, and Apply

Discover how the I-System causes your cravings and leads to relapse.

Experience how tuning in to your senses reduces cravings and urges.

Apply your recovery tools in your daily life.

Mind-Body Language

I-System: Each of us has an I-System, and it's either active (on) or resting (off). When it's on, it creates dysfunction in your mind-body. You know the I-System is on when your mind is cluttered with spinning thoughts, your body is tense, your awareness is contracted, and your mental and physical functioning is impaired. It's called the I-System because it prompts you to falsely identify with the spinning thoughts and the physical distress it causes.

Addicted mode: Addiction is best understood as a specific, habitual, and temporal way of existing, relating, and living, which is characterized by habitual substance abuse and loss of control.

True self: How you think, feel, see the world, and act when your I-System is resting. Your true self is always present in the natural functioning state, where your mind and body work in harmony, as a healing unit.

Damaged self: How you think, feel, see the world, and act when your I-System is active. Life is overwhelming, your natural functioning is impaired, and you struggle to control your addicted mode.

Mind-body bridging: When you use the tools in this workbook, you form a bridge from your damaged self with an active I-System to your true self in the natural functioning state, which handles daily life in a smooth and healthy way.

LEARN HOW TO MANAGE YOUR CRAVINGS

There are many reasons why you relapse—even when you have made the commitment to stay abstinent. One of the primary reasons for relapse is that recovering addicts do not have the necessary coping skills to manage cravings. Cravings have been described as one of the major factors related to relapse (Marlatt and Gordon 1985). Consequently, your ability to manage cravings is a pivotal skill needed for your sustained recovery from your addiction. This chapter of the book will provide answers to your questions and help you to see what lies at the root of your struggles with addiction.

The mind-body bridging recovery tools that you will learn and experience while doing the written exercises in this workbook will provide you with simple, yet powerful tools to manage your cravings. These powerful recovery tools will work within the first ten minutes of doing the exercises in this workbook and will rapidly begin to transform your life. Recent research and clinical experience has shown that the therapeutic effect of mind-body bridging in domestic violence perpetrators, veterans, and cancer survivors (Tollefson et al. 2009; Nakamura et al. 2011; Nakamura et al. 2013) is powerful and has a very rapid onset (within the first week of treatment). Furthermore, research has shown that three weekly sessions of mind-body bridging reduce the salivary enzyme alpha-amylase, a non-invasive biological marker of stress (Lipschitz et al. 2013). Preliminary findings suggest that the neuropeptide (hormone) oxytocin, which has a calming and bonding function in humans with implications for improving well-being, showed an increase in response after three sessions of MBB (Lipschitz et al. 2015). Improvements in well-being were also associated with reductions in cravings and addictions following an MBB intervention targeting substance abuse in a residential population undergoing usual care (Nakamura et al. 2015). Thus, MBB could serve as an effective intervention program to help reduce levels of biomarkers of stress and increase those of well-being in a variety of clinical populations, including people struggling with drug addiction.

The next two exercises will help you to see what lies at the root of your struggles with cravings and urges. Think of the most troubling situation in which you experience cravings and an urge to use (for example, going to a social event). Write the situation in the oval below. It may be helpful to look at the sample map on the next page. Now, take a couple of minutes to write down around the oval any thoughts that come to mind about that situation. Be as specific as possible. Work quickly, without self-editing.

TROUBLING SITUATION MAP

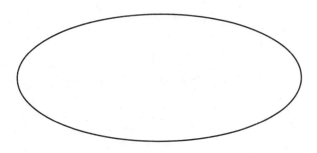

A. Is your mind clear or cluttered with thoughts?

_____

B. Is your body tense or relaxed? List where and how your body is tense:

_____

_____

C. With your mind and body in this condition, how do you feel and act?

_____

SAMPLE MAP: TROUBLING SITUATION

I will be boring.

Can't cope.

Fearful I will take a drink.

What if somebody offers me alcohol?

Cravings will be unbearable.

BEING AT A SOCIAL EVENT

I feel nervous and awkward without drinking or using at a social event.

Feel lost without using.

A. Is your mind clear or cluttered with thoughts?

My mind is cluttered with anxious thoughts and cravings.

B. Is your body tense or relaxed? List where and how your body is tense:

Band around my head, hard to breathe, really tense all over.

C. With your mind and body in this condition, how do you feel and act?

Anxious—avoid social events at all costs.

EXPERIENCE HOW TO REDUCE CRAVINGS

For this exercise, it is helpful to be in a room without distractions, such as people talking, TV, or electronic devices. Write down the same situation (the one you wrote in the oval on the first map) in the oval below. Before you continue, seat yourself comfortably, listen to any background sounds, feel the pressure of your body on your seat, feel your feet on the floor, and feel the pen in your hand. Take your time. If you have thoughts, gently return to listening to the background sounds and tuning in to your senses. Once you feel settled, start writing whatever comes to mind about the situation. Watch the ink go onto the paper, keep feeling the pen in your hand, and listen to the background sounds. Write for a couple of minutes.

TROUBLING SITUATION MAP WITH BRIDGING

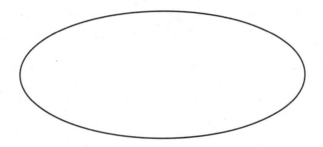

A. Is your mind clear or cluttered with thoughts?

_____

B. Is your body tense or relaxed?

_____

C. How is this map different from the first one you made?

_____

If this second map is not different, find a quiet room, and take your time as you follow the above instructions while you do the map again.

D. How would you feel and act in this mind-body state?

_____

E. If you could live your life with your mind-body in this state, do you think your life would be better?
Yes _____   No _____

The exercises that you have just completed are called *mind-body maps*. *Mind-body mapping* consists of short written exercises which take no longer than a few minutes and give you an accurate picture of how your mind and body work.

Now, look at your first map. Do most of the items listed clutter your mind with thoughts and fill your body with tension? You probably think it's the situation that's creating the inner distress and cravings you see on your map. It's not! You have just experienced your active Identity System (I-System). We all have a system in our bodies called the Identity System. The I-System takes a particular situation, creates mind clutter and body tension, and limits our ability to act optimally. When your I-System is active, it limits your choices to a few habitual patterns. Your I-System causes commotion—tension in your body, clutter in your mind—and impairs how you live your life. This commotion machine creates so much static that it paralyzes you when you try to carry out your best intentions. Your cravings and urges run your life. Your I-System disconnects you from your innate wellspring of wisdom, power, healing, and goodness.

Take a look at your two completed maps. Your first map shows your I-System in action. In your second map, you got to see what it's like to have a quiet I-System. You just experienced a dramatic shift in your mind-body state, from your I-System to your true self. Notice how your body relaxed and your mind became clearer on the second map. When you literally come to your senses by focusing on your body sensations and the sounds around you, the I-System automatically quiets, your body tension eases, and your cravings are reduced. The reality of the situation is still the same, but your relationship toward it is different.

All the physiological, psychological, and social issues (genetics, upbringing, difficult experiences, or mistakes) that contribute to your addiction (Du Plessis 2012, 2015) have one thing in common: they feed your I-System. And in the here-and-now, all overpowering cravings are I-System-driven. Therefore, to manage cravings in the here-and-now, all that is required is for you to recognize your I-System and put it to rest as you go about the activities of daily living.

Whenever you have the specific body tension and unpleasant body sensations you experienced on the first map, you know your I-System is active. Mind-body bridging uses the mind and the body to move you from a state with limited choices, to a place where you have a wider range of options.

ADDICTED MODE

Addiction is best understood as a *mode of being* (or *mode* for short), meaning that it is a particular and habitual way of existing, relating, and living. You will experience in this workbook that all aspects related to your *addicted mode* (thoughts, emotions, attitudes, beliefs, and behaviors) are the result of an overactive I-System.

In this workbook you will experience that your addiction is not a permanent or chronic condition, but rather a transitory mode that is one of many possible modes of being. You are much more than just your addicted mode. Your addiction can only function when your I-System is active. Once the I-System is active, you live your daily life fearful of relapse, as if your mind, body, and world are your enemies. By doing the exercises in this workbook, you will learn how to use your innate ability to manage your I-System, thereby gaining freedom from your addiction.

YOU ARE MORE THAN YOUR ADDICTION

Cravings and urges are elements that are part of certain habitual thoughts, emotions, attitudes, beliefs, and behaviors. They are a natural and unavoidable aspect of any recovery process. In themselves, cravings are not dangerous or problematic. The problem is that when cravings are captured by your I-System, they become amplified and experienced in a very destructive way, and eventually lead to a relapse. Like all thoughts and emotions, cravings will naturally fade away by quieting the I-System. Cravings are thus best understood on a *continuum*. On the one side are cravings that are not captured by your I-System, which naturally arise and fade. Then there are cravings that are captured by your I-System that range in various degrees of intensity. On the far side of the craving continuum, your mind-body is so consumed by the cravings that all rational functioning breaks down and relapse seems like the only option available to you. In this state, you have become so identified with an I-System-captured craving that you just give in to it. By using mind-body bridging, you manage your cravings naturally and harmlessly. Remember, it is only when cravings are captured by the I-System that they become problematic.

When you did the first map, you were full of cravings, urges, troubling thoughts, and body tension, and you didn't have enough room left to experience your self-healing power. When you quiet your I-System, as you did in the second map, you become more settled and better able to handle situations in a healthy way (as shown in figure 1.1 on the next page).

Using three vessels—a one-ounce shot glass, a twelve-ounce water glass, and a thirty-two-ounce vase—as a metaphor, you can personally measure how you are dealing with your urges and cravings. Imagine the one-ounce shot glass filled to the top with cravings, troubling thoughts, and body tension. This vessel is so full there is no room for change. Your existence is nothing but an addictive mode. In this state, you are completely identified as a damaged self, and in this state your choices are reduced to limited and habitual behaviors.

When you are overcome by your urges and cravings, you experience yourself as a small and limited vessel, a damaged self, trapped within an addicted mode. Your ability to handle cravings and urges (the darkly shaded space) is greatly limited. You have falsely come to believe that the small vessel, an addicted mode, is all you are. This allows you to only use a fraction of your self-healing power (the lightly shaded area). When your I-System is active, you feel limited and stuck. This stops you from being able to manage your addiction, and greatly limits your choices. From an existential perspective, you perceive yourself as an isolated and alienated individual, with no authentic relation to others and the world.

When you quiet your I-System, like you did on the second map, you expand your capacity—it's like pouring your one ounce of cravings and urges into a twelve-ounce vessel. Even though the same amount of cravings and urges are present, there is now space for change and for more choices. The extra space is your wellspring of healing, goodness, and wisdom. Now take the twelve-ounce container and pour it into the largest vessel. What happens? The urges and cravings are still there, but they barely cover the bottom of the vessel. The largest vessel's expanded available space represents your true self. The situation hasn't changed, but the space inside the vessel has changed. You may still experience urges and cravings, but as your true self they are experienced as fleeting phenomena, like any thoughts or feelings. With mind-body bridging you become greater than any of your cravings and urges. You can now begin to deal with troubling situations quickly and in a healthy way, without your cravings being amplified and leading to relapse. Keep in mind that you don't have to force yourself to function naturally; this skill will develop on its own. It is your birthright. When you begin resting your I-System, your senses come to life, your mind becomes clearer and open, and your body relaxes. Using mind-body bridging tools, you begin to experience the vastness of who you really are. When you are the big vessel (true self), you have the capacity and power to handle your urges and cravings.

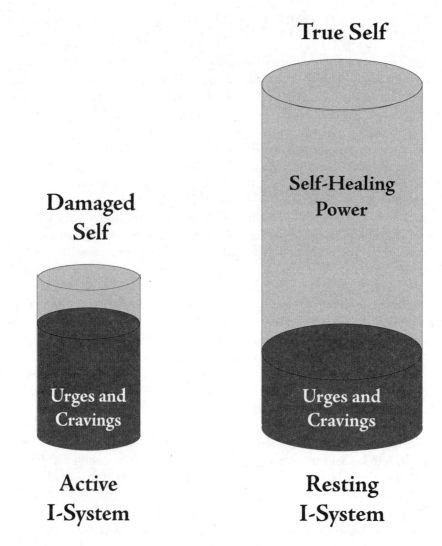

Figure 1.1 Which vessel are you in?

The bigger vessel, representing your true self, is referred to in 12-step programs as a *Higher Power* or *Higher Self*-aligned state of being. You have expanded your existence beyond your addicted mode, represented by the smaller vessel. In the *Big Book* of Alcoholics Anonymous, it is written that at the root of alcoholism is "self-centered fear." As we have seen, this contracted state of self-centered fear is due to your active I-System. In this state you see yourself as the small vessel, and you come to falsely believe that the one-ounce shot glass is all you are.

MBB QUALITY OF LIFE GAUGE

Date: _____

It's time to fill out your first MBB Quality of Life Gauge. This scale is repeated throughout the workbook so that you can measure the impact that this book has on the quality of your life. Think back over the past week as you fill out the chart.

Circle the number under your answer.	Not at all	Several days	More than half the days	Nearly every day
1. I've had positive interest and pleasure in my activities.	0	1	3	5
2. I've felt optimistic, excited, and hopeful.	0	1	3	5
3. I've slept well and woken up feeling refreshed.	0	1	3	5
4. I've had lots of energy.	0	1	3	5
5. I've been able to focus on tasks and use self-discipline.	0	1	3	5
6. I've stayed healthy, eaten well, exercised, and had fun.	0	1	3	5
7. I've felt good about my relationships with my family and friends.	0	1	3	5
8. I've been satisfied with my accomplishments at home, work, or school.	0	1	3	5
9. I've been comfortable with my financial situation.	0	1	3	5
10. I've felt good about the spiritual base of my life.	0	1	3	5
11. I've been satisfied with the direction of my life.	0	1	3	5
12. I've felt fulfilled, with a sense of well-being and peace of mind.	0	1	3	5

Score Key: Column Total   ____   ____   ____   ____

0–15 . . . . Poor

16–30 . . . . Fair   Total Score _____

31–45 . . . . Good

46 and above . . . . Excellent

RECOVERY TOOLS

Remember the mapping exercise? When you did the first map, you explored a situation that triggered a craving. The second map allowed you to explore that same situation with a calmer body and clearer mind. Maybe this state lasted for a while, or maybe it was brief. When you made your second map, what pulled you away from hearing the background sounds, feeling the pen, and seeing the ink go onto the paper? Yes, it was your thoughts. The I-System spins your thoughts, makes your body tense, and closes you off from your senses. It converts troubling situations into inner distress and often cravings.

Thought labeling and bridging awareness practices are the recovery tools you will learn in this chapter to reduce your cravings. Apart from craving reduction and relapse prevention, the recovery tools in this book will help you build resilience in all aspects of your recovery lifestyle. In this chapter we specifically focus on craving reduction and relapse prevention, and in later chapters you will learn how to use these tools to improve all aspects of your recovery.

Thought Labeling

Your mind naturally makes both positive and negative thoughts. You will never get rid of your negative thoughts. In fact, trying to get rid of them doesn't work, because when you push them away, you give them even more energy, adding to your distress.

A significant feature of being in an addicted mode is the habitual thinking patterns associated with it. These habitual thinking patterns, often referred to as "stinking thinking" in recovery culture, are typically characterized by negative and destructive thoughts that reinforce your substance abuse. Addictive thinking patterns, or "stinking thinking," are often present when you are experiencing cravings and urges. Moreover, these patterns can frequently lead to relapse. Examples of addictive thinking patterns are denial, rationalization, blame, self-pity, self-obsession, projection, and many others. It isn't the content of your thoughts or even the thinking pattern that is important to recovery; it is the fact that all thoughts are just thoughts. When craving thoughts come up, label them using a recovery tool called *thought labeling*. Thought labeling lets you see that a thought is *just a thought*. This prevents the I-System from taking a thought, spinning a story from it, crossing the mind-body connection, and creating a craving-filled body. Once that happens, the thought is no longer just a thought, but a state of mind-body distress. Thoughts belong in our minds, not our bodies.

Let's see how thought labeling works. From the first map you did earlier, select a specific thought associated with a lot of body tension; for example, *How will I be able to go on a date sober?* Since the thought causes body tension, it means your I-System captured that thought. The thought has become boss, and you have become its servant. Now look at that selected thought, sense your body tension, and say to yourself, *I'm having the thought, "How will I be able to go on a date sober?"* Some people even add *and a thought is just a thought*. Continue to label that thought until you experience a reduction of body tension. This recognition that a thought is just a thought is one of the tools that will help you stop your I-System from capturing thoughts. When the I-System doesn't grab your thoughts, your true self in the natural functioning state handles the situation without you going into an addicted mode.

Rex was a thirty-five-year-old business executive who seemed to have it all together. He had been in recovery for two years, but before presenting his ideas at board meetings, he was plagued with intense feelings of self-doubt, which often led to cravings. Previously, he coped by having a couple of lines of cocaine before a board meeting to boost his self-confidence. After learning about mind-body bridging, he started using thought labeling to quiet the spin of his I-System. Now when he has the thought, *The board is going to hate my ideas,* he labels it as *I am having a thought, "The board is going to hate my ideas."* This has greatly helped Rex to manage his anxiety and self-doubt, thereby reducing his cravings. Rex was able to see and fully experience that it was not his presenting to the board or his concern about rejection that caused his self-doubt and anxiety; it was the paralysis caused by his I-System making him falsely believe that he was incapable of handling whatever the board would do. He was amazed at the power that his thoughts had over him. As time went on, he came to smile at his thoughts because he saw the truth; a thought was just a thought.

Use thought labeling to reduce your cravings. During the day, when craving thoughts pull you away from what you are doing, label the thoughts and go back to your activity. For example, when you're in the shower, and the thought *I will never get through the day* pops into your mind, say to yourself, *I am having the thought, "I'll never get through the day,"* return to taking your shower, sense the water on your body, and hear the sounds of the shower. Each time you do that, you reduce the power of your I-System and gain more access to your wellspring of healing, goodness, and wisdom.

Bridging Awareness Practices

When the I-System is active, it closes off your senses until all you are aware of is your cravings, troubling thoughts, and body tension. It's like putting your hands over your ears to block out sounds. The I-System not only keeps you from hearing the background sounds around you, but also keeps you from experiencing your ever-present self-healing powers. Your cravings and urges are all that matter. When you use your senses, your I-System quiets, letting you deal with your challenges with a calm, ready mind and a relaxed body. Bridging awareness practices use your senses to build a bridge from a life filled with cravings and urges (run by the damaged self of the I-System) to a life lived at its best (run by the true self of natural functioning).

There are many mindfulness-based techniques that are used in addiction treatment to expand awareness. While awareness training exercises have many benefits, from a mind-body bridging perspective, the core issue of awareness is to free it from the I-System's domination. From an I-System perspective, there are two types of awareness: I-System-captured awareness (damaged self), and awareness with a resting I-System (true self). Contracted awareness is a consequence of an active I-System. When your I-System is active, your awareness automatically contracts, leading to a fragmented view of reality. For instance, the mechanism of denial, which is one of the primary obstacles to recovery, is in essence the result of I-System-captured awareness. This in turn leads to a fragmented understanding of the harm done by one's addiction, perpetuating the addiction even more. When the I-System is quiet, awareness expands naturally and automatically. Therefore the aim of mind-body bridging is not to expand awareness, as expanded awareness is your natural state, but rather to manage the internal mechanism (I-System) that causes contracted awareness. When your true self is in charge, you have the natural ability to heal from your addiction. Rather than focusing on skills to expand awareness, mind-body bridging focuses on the cause of collapsed awareness, the I-System.

AWARENESS OF BACKGROUND SOUNDS

Your environment is full of sounds. During the day, pause and listen to any background sounds, like the white noise of the heating or air-conditioning system, the wind blowing, traffic sounds, or the hum of the refrigerator. If your thoughts start to spin, label them and gently return your awareness to what you were doing. See what happens to your mind and body when you focus on background sounds.

Colette, twenty-four years old, is a recovering sedative and sleeping tablet addict. One of her biggest triggers for relapse had always been her lifelong struggle with insomnia. She would go to bed fearful that she would not sleep, and her mind-body would be tense with out-of-control and anxious thoughts. Her therapist suggested mind-body bridging exercises for her to do when going to bed. Colette lived near the sea, and when she felt her body tense up and her thoughts begin to spin, she would focus on the sound of the waves. She reported to her therapist a week later that her sleeping pattern had significantly improved. Now, she routinely listens to the background sounds, whatever they are and wherever she is. Colette reports that her days are filled with less tension.

AWARENESS OF WHAT YOU ARE TOUCHING

We all touch hundreds of things every day. Were you aware of how it felt under your fingertips today when you touched your shoes, socks, shirt, keys, fork, watch, paper, cell phone, or computer? Were you aware of your senses when you touched your child or a close friend? Did you sense the warmth of the coffee cup or the coldness of the water bottle in your hand? Chances are you didn't. Your I-System has numbed your body, detaching you from your senses. Tuning in to your sense of touch is another bridging awareness practice that quiets your I-System and strengthens your self-healing power.

Be aware of what the sensations are as you touch things like glasses, phones, pens, keys, or computers. Are these surfaces smooth or rough, cold or warm, pleasant or unpleasant? When washing your hands or showering, feel the water as it touches your skin. Sense what it's like to touch others or be touched. This may take some effort, because the I-System dulls your senses. Note what you touch and the sensations you feel during the day. Do you feel more settled when you are aware of what you are touching? Keep practicing!

AWARENESS OF COLORS, FACIAL FEATURES, AND SHAPES

The I-System grasps at certain images while rejecting others. This prevents you from seeing the whole picture. When you use one or more of your senses, the I-System calms down, your awareness expands, and you actually see what's out there. When you look at a sunset or even a speck of dust on the floor, does your busy head let you see its colors, shapes, and uniqueness? Probably not for long. Take a look at your next meal. When your food is in front of you, really look at it before you eat. What textures are there? What are the shapes? What color is your food?

Chris had been in recovery from cocaine addiction for five years. After being clean for two years, he developed a gambling problem. Whenever he walked past the news vendor and saw lottery tickets for sale, his mind would fill with spinning thoughts and intense cravings to play the lottery. Using his newly acquired bridging awareness practices, he would focus on the shapes and textures of the sidewalk and sense the pressure on his feet as he was walking past the vendor. This greatly helped him to manage his cravings until they eventually disappeared.

Pay attention today to what you see when you look at scenery and objects. Notice their colors, shapes, and forms. Pay attention to the facial expressions of the people around you, like family, friends, coworkers, and even strangers. When you have an addictive thought, label it as just a thought, and gently return to whatever you were doing. When you really see your surroundings, your I-System quiets, and your appreciation of life expands as your cravings fade.

AWARENESS OF YOUR BODY SENSATIONS

Awareness of how your body feels is an important part of your ability to reduce cravings and urges. Because of the unpleasant body sensations associated with your cravings, you may have developed a habit of trying to block out or get away from the feelings in your body. You may get away from those unpleasant feelings for a little while, but avoiding your body sensations prevents your self-healing of addiction. When you have unpleasant body sensations, expand your awareness to all parts of your body, and pay particular attention to your senses and the sensations of the things you touch. Your expanded awareness means you have expanded your self-healing powers.

The proprioceptive system is a vital part of your nervous system that informs you about your posture, the way you move, and the degree to which your muscles contract. The tense muscles you noticed when you did your first map were due to the I-System getting in the way of the natural functioning of the proprioceptive system. Your natural functioning is signaling for the muscles to relax, but your I-System takes over that normal response and tightens up the muscles even further. This is an example of how the I-System works to disrupt mind-body harmony. Another example is responding to an injury that causes pain. Acute pain is a signal to take action right away. After a few minutes, the central nervous system sets up a barrier to reduce the pain signals, so that you are better able to carry on with your daily life. In many people with chronic pain, the I-System removes the barrier so that the intense pain remains for weeks, months, or even years, getting in the way of their daily lives and things they need to do.

Let's see how this works. Start leaning slowly to the left. Do you feel the muscle tension in your side? Do you sense the imbalance in your head? Do you sense how your natural functioning wants to correct the imbalance? Lift up your right arm and hold it in midair. Do you feel the pull of gravity? Yes, that's your proprioceptive system at work. It gives you information about the position of your body in space and the state of your muscles. You use that natural flow of information to automatically move and navigate. Pay attention to gravity as you lift an object or as you get up from a chair. Gravity is your friend; it's always there. Sensing gravity quiets the I-System and grounds you in the present moment.

REVIEW

Discover

- That mind clutter and body tension are associated with your cravings and urges.

- That a clear mind and a relaxed, ready body are associated with your natural functioning.

Experience

- Mind clutter and body tension are caused by an active I-System. It is a counterproductive system in your brain (present in all of us) that falsely causes you to experience yourself as damaged and is the core of your addiction. Whenever you experience unpleasant body sensations like the ones on the first map earlier in this chapter, it is a red flag that your I-System is active.

- When you use the recovery tools in this workbook, you form a bridge from your damaged self with an active I-System to your true self in the naturally functioning state, which handles daily life in a smooth and healthy way.

Apply

- Use your recovery tools to manage your cravings, stay relaxed, and stay focused throughout the day. When your thoughts begin to wander from what you are doing, label them as just thoughts, and then bring your attention back to the activity. When you first start to experience cravings (as you did in the first map) or feel yourself shifting into an addicted mode, use your bridging awareness tools. Notice how your body automatically relaxes and your breathing becomes natural without your having to force it. You are now in direct communication with your mind-body. For example, while you are at work, listen to background sounds like a ticking clock or the hum of your computer, and you will find that your other senses automatically open. As you listen to these sounds, your sense of calm expands.

- As you are falling asleep tonight, listen to and focus on background sounds. Feel and rub the sheets with your fingers. See the darkness when your eyes are closed. Be patient and keep returning to your senses. The busy head can never settle the busy head. If thoughts that can lead to cravings (*I have to meet new people tomorrow*) keep you awake, label your thoughts; for example, say to yourself, *I'm having the thought, "I have to meet new people tomorrow"* or *I'm having the thought, "I hate meeting new people, so what else is new?"* and then return to your senses and fall asleep. These recovery tools (using your senses and thought labeling) stop the activities of the I-System from robbing you of a restful sleep. The quality of your sleep is an important component in healing from your addiction. Improving sleep using mind-body bridging is very effective (Nakamura et al. 2011; Nakamura et al. 2013; Nakamura et al. 2015).

Recovery Tools

➤ Recognize when your I-System is active (on) or inactive (off).

➤ Thought labeling

➤ Bridging awareness practices:

- Awareness of background sounds

- Awareness of what you are touching

- Awareness of colors, facial features, and shapes

- Awareness of your body sensations

You may ask yourself, *Can labeling my thoughts, listening to background sounds, seeing facial features, feeling my feet on the ground, and being aware of what I touch really help me reduce my cravings and live a better life? Can it really be so simple?* When you make a habit of using these tools for reducing cravings, all the cells in your body will give you a resounding yes! So, feel your foot as it touches the ground, sense your fingers on the computer keys, hear the background sounds, feel the pressure on your behind as you sit, feel the fork in your hand, look at your food, and be aware of how the broom moves the dust when you sweep. When your troubling thoughts pull you away from what you are doing, label them and return to the activity.

After using these tools for a couple of days, return to this page. Fill out the following chart, and then the MBB Rating Scale that is on the next page.

Difficult Situation	I-System: Active or Inactive	Thought Labeling	Bridging Awareness Tools	What Happened
Thinking about having a busy day while showering	Active	I'm having the thought "I won't be able to manage."	Paid attention to the sounds of the shower.	Tension dropped, able to calmly get ready.
Having a heated discussion	Active	I'm having the thought "I need to be in control."	Listened to the sounds of the air conditioner system. Paid attention to the facial features of the other person.	Became more relaxed and discussion went smoothly.

Have you noticed that besides reducing cravings, using these tools as part of your daily routine helps you to enjoy life more and be more productive? These tools for reducing cravings serve as the basis for the entire workbook. The stronger your mind-body bridging practices, the easier it will be to prevent relapse and build recovery resilience. The following MBB Rating Scale is a way to gauge your progress that lets you know how solid your foundation is.

MBB RATING SCALE: COME TO YOUR SENSES AND OVERCOME CRAVINGS

Date: _____

After using the tools in this chapter for several days, check the box below that best describes your practice for each question: hardly ever, sometimes, usually, or almost always.

How often do you...	Hardly Ever	Sometimes	Usually	Almost Always
Listen to background sounds?				
Sense the sensations in your fingers when holding your water bottle, a coffee cup, a cold glass of water, or a soda can?				
Sense the sensations in your fingers when you touch things throughout the day?				
Experience pressure on your feet when you walk?				
Experience pressure on your behind as you sit?				
Feel the steering wheel, hear the roar of the engine, and pay attention to the road when you are driving?				
Hear the water going down the drain and feel it on your body when you shower or wash your hands?				
Become keenly aware of daily activities like making the bed, eating, brushing your teeth, and lifting?				
Become aware of your body sensations when you touch others?				
Become keenly aware of others' facial expressions?				
Use recovery tools to help you manage situations at home and at work?				
Use bridging awareness and thought labeling tools to help you sleep?				
Use recovery tools to reduce cravings?				
Sense that you are connected to your own wellspring of healing, goodness, and wisdom?				
Know when your I-System is active (on) or inactive (off)?				

List two new things you've noticed about your life after starting to use your recovery tools:

_____

_____

CHAPTER 2

DEAL EFFECTIVELY WITH HIGH-RISK SITUATIONS

Discover, Experience, and Apply

Discover how requirements ignite your cravings and urges.

Experience how your requirements are triggered.

Apply your recovery tools in your daily life.

Mind-Body Language

Requirements: Thoughts made into mental rules by your I-System that tell how you and the world should be in each moment. When your I-System rules are not met, you become filled with body tension and troubling thoughts. Unmet requirements will always put you in the addicted mode.

Recognize requirements: When you become clearly aware that your requirement—not the events around you—is making your I-System active, you curtail the activity of your I-System and begin self-healing in a natural functioning state.

HOW THE I-SYSTEM WORKS

A lot of systems regulate our bodies. For instance, we have a system that regulates our temperature, keeping the body at around 98.6 degrees Fahrenheit. If our temperature goes up, we sweat, and if it goes down, we shiver, as our system tries to get back to the body's normal temperature. In the same way, we all have an I-System. It works like the system that regulates our temperature, but instead of an ideal temperature, the I-System creates an ideal picture (*requirement*) of how you and the world should be. Each moment, both systems sense whether their requirements are met. When the requirement of the system that regulates temperature is not fulfilled, we shiver or sweat. When something comes up that doesn't fulfill the I-System requirement, our I-System becomes active: our body gets tense, our mind becomes cluttered, and we enter the addictive mode. The natural state of the I-System is to rest. It's only turned on when requirements are unfulfilled. Remember, requirements are rules that your I-System has created for you about how you and the world should be at any moment; for example, *I should be able to control my cravings*; *I shouldn't have negative thoughts*; *My partner should be more understanding*.

It's vital to know the difference between thoughts that are *natural expectations* and those that are captured by the I-System and made into requirements. All thoughts are natural and start free of the I-System's influence. It's not a thought's content but what happens to the thought that makes it a requirement. For example, *I don't like it when my boss criticizes me* is a thought or expectation you may naturally have. The I-System works by taking that natural thought and creating an ideal picture of how you and the world should be (*People should not criticize each other*). To do that, it takes the natural expectation and turns it into a requirement: *My boss should not criticize me*. You can tell it's a requirement because you have excess body tension and mental stress whenever the situation (your boss criticizing you) violates the rule or demand of the requirement. When a thought is not a requirement, you still have your natural expectation, but your mind is clear, your body is relaxed, and your true self is in charge. You now deal more effectively with anything that may come up.

It's crucial to continually recognize whether or not your I-System is active, and it's important to notice that whenever the I-System captures a natural thought or expectation and makes it into a requirement, you become a victim of circumstances because your ability to act freely is handicapped. This chapter gives you the tools to quiet your I-System, regain your natural functioning, and heal from your addiction.

DISCOVER HOW REQUIREMENTS PREVENT SELF-HEALING

It's time to start mapping your I-System requirements. Remember that the two-part mind-body maps are short written exercises that take only a few minutes. They're vivid pictures of your thoughts and body tension. Every two-part map you create makes you more aware of your requirements, reduces control by your I-System, and helps you manage high-risk situations.

This mapping exercise is a powerful way to uncover requirements that sap your ability to live your best life. Do a How My World Should Be map (see the following sample map). Take a few minutes to write around the oval any thoughts that you have about how your everyday world should be; for example, *My partner should understand what I am going through,* or *I shouldn't be afraid,* or *I should have more money.* Be specific and work quickly, without editing your thoughts. See the example map.

HOW MY WORLD SHOULD BE MAP

HOW MY WORLD SHOULD BE

SAMPLE MAP: HOW MY WORLD SHOULD BE

People should not blame
me for my addiction.

I shouldn't have those
recurring troubling thoughts.

I should not be
an addict.

I should not have cravings.

My partner should understand
what I am going through.

I should be in control
of my using.

HOW MY WORLD SHOULD BE

My parents should have gotten
me the help I needed.

My recovery should be better.

My house should be the
way I like it.

I should wash my car.

My family should accept
me as I am.

A. Do you think everything on your map will happen?   Yes _____   No _____

B. In this chart, write down each thought and describe your body tension when you realized that it might **not** happen.

"How My World Should Be" Thought	Body Tension and Location	
Example 1: *My family should accept me as I am.*	*Churning stomach, palpitations*	√
Example 2: *I should wash my car.*	*Minimal body tension*	

C. The body tension you listed is a sign that the thought is a requirement and has activated your I-System. Place a check mark in the third column to indicate that the particular thought is a requirement.

We all have natural thoughts about how the world should be. When your I-System takes hold of these thoughts and you see that they might not happen, your body tenses and your mind gets cluttered. This sets the stage for you to move into an addicted mode.

Remember, thoughts that turn on your I-System are requirements. In the previous example, take the thought *My family should accept me*. When you have the thought *My family should accept me as I am*, your stomach churns, your heart pounds, and your thoughts spin. This means you have the requirement *My family should accept me as I am*, and your requirement is interfering with your natural ability to cope with that situation in a healthy way. If your I-System hadn't captured that thought, it would have remained a natural expectation. You would then relate to your family with a relaxed body and a clear mind, whether or not your family accepted you. For the other thought listed as an example (*I should wash my car*), you have minimal body tension when reality doesn't match that thought. In this case, your I-System is not triggered, so the thought *I should wash my car* isn't a requirement; it's a natural thought. It means that you'll still have a relaxed body and a clear mind whether or not you wash your car.

BEGIN TO EXPERIENCE HOW TO SELF-HEAL YOUR ADDICTION

Now you'll use the bridging awareness practices you learned in chapter 1 and do a How My World Should Be map again. Before you start writing, listen to any background sounds, experience your body's pressure on your seat, sense your feet on the floor, and feel the pen in your hand. Take your time. Once you feel settled, keep feeling the pen in your hand and start writing about how your world should be. Watch the ink go onto the paper, and listen to any background sounds. For the next few minutes, jot down whatever comes to mind about how the world should be.

HOW MY WORLD SHOULD BE MAP WITH BRIDGING

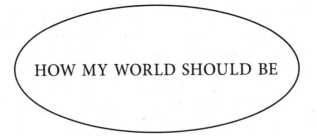

HOW MY WORLD SHOULD BE

A. What are the differences between this map and the previous map?

_____

_____

B. Do you see that you can face your world as it is, without having the extra pressure of your I-System, as is shown on the previous map you made?   Yes _____   No _____

When you encounter an event or a thought (like *I should be in control of my using*) that fills your mind with spinning thoughts and tenses your body, you know it's your I-System making you feel distressed. If you recognize your requirement and tune in to your senses, you will quiet your I-System and be in better control of your using. Your mind clutter and body tension will soon reduce and you will handle what's happening with a ready, relaxed mind and body.

Whenever you have body tension (unpleasant body sensations) and mind clutter (troubling thoughts), it's a sign that one of your I-System requirements is not being fulfilled. You are at risk of entering into an addicted mode. The mapping exercise you just did is about recognizing your requirements. Notice your signs of an active I-System. For example, maybe your shoulders start to rise, your stomach churns, you feel overwhelmed, your breathing changes, you stop hearing the fan, or you slump in your chair. Once you notice a sign, see if you can find the requirement that activated your I-System. When you identify your requirement, you have more control over what's upsetting you. Remember, it is not the situation or another person's behavior that activates your I-System; it's your own requirement.

HIGH-RISK SITUATIONS AND REQUIREMENTS

High-risk situations are internal or external events that have the potential to trigger cravings and urges to use. Each person has a unique set of high-risk situations related to his or her life situation and past experience of addiction. For instance, a high-risk situation for a cigarette smoker could be the moment he or she walks out of a movie theater or directly after dinner. For a cocaine addict, a high-risk situation could be going to a party or function. Although each person has a unique set of high-risk situations, generally the three most common types of high-risk situations are 1) negative or challenging emotional states, 2) social pressure, and 3) interpersonal conflict (Bowen, Chawla, and Marlatt 2011).

As a recovering addict, it is impossible to avoid all high-risk situations and their associated triggers. It is imperative, for ongoing sobriety, to learn to manage these situations. At the root of any craving-triggering situation lies an I-System requirement. Therefore, to successfully manage or defuse high-risk situations, you need to learn how to recognize the I-System requirement underlying the situation. This prevents the I-System from spinning out of control. Remember, it's not your natural expectation (for people to be kind) that is the problem, but that the I-System has captured that natural expectation and made it into an I-System requirement (*People should be kind*). Then when people are unkind, your I-System activates and you enter an addicted mode. If it were just a natural expectation, your I-System would not be activated and your true self would handle the situation in an effective and healthy way (natural functioning).

12-step programs traditionally place a strong emphasis on the danger of expectations of ourselves, others, and the world, as well as working through resentments. In fellowship meetings, it is often said, "Expectations are premeditated resentments." From a mind-body bridging perspective, at the root of each resentment lies an unmet I-System requirement that strengthens your addicted mode. So, when you are faced with a situation that triggers your requirements, your I-System activates and an addicted mode results. The more requirements you have, the more chance that your I-System will get activated. The 12-step programs point out that resentment is one of the leading causes of relapse. From a mind-body bridging perspective, it is clear why resentments pose such a risk for ongoing sobriety. As you will see when doing the following exercises, it is not the nature of the situation that makes it high risk; it's the violation of requirements about the situation that leads to an overactive I-System with cravings and urges. The aim of mind-body bridging is not to change the situation but instead to change the way you relate to the situation. In other words, you'll learn to deal with the situation without going into an addicted mode, and with a quiet I-System.

MANAGING HIGH-RISK SITUATIONS

The existence of high-risk situations is an unavoidable aspect of any recovering addict's life. Doing mind-body mapping prepares you to face these situations without melting down. In this exercise, you work with a current high-risk situation that could lead to powerful cravings or possibly relapse. In the first map you identify the requirements connected to the situation. The second map lets you feel the mind-body shift from an active I-System (addicted mode) to an I-System at rest (natural functioning state). Mapping reins in your addiction and allows you to function in a natural way.

1. Do a High-Risk Situation map. In the oval below, write down a current high-risk situation. Next, take a couple of minutes to write around the oval any thoughts that come to mind. Work quickly, without editing your thoughts. At the bottom of the map, carefully describe the areas of your body that are tense. Next, place a check mark next to each item with body tension.

HIGH-RISK SITUATION MAP

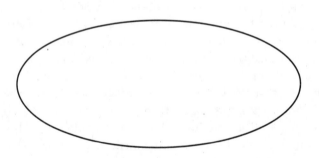

Body Tension: _____

_____

What does your map say about how you are approaching the situation?

A. Is your mind cluttered or clear?

_____

Recognizing the start of the tension in your body is a basic first step in recognizing when you are about to enter into an addicted mode.

B. Sense what your body feels like when you are beginning to crave. Note where and how your body tension increases as your cravings and urges build. Describe your buildup of body tension:

_____

_____

_____

C. How would you feel and act in this state?

_____

_____

_____

Your body always has tension or negative body sensations before your cravings become full-blown and you enter into an addicted mode. No matter what you are thinking, excessive cravings and being in an addicted mode are not possible with a relaxed body.

Recognizing your requirements is crucial to managing your addicted mode. Look at what you wrote in the oval (for example, *My wife argues with me*) and discover your requirement by asking yourself how that item "should" be (*She should not argue with me*). Do the same for each item (*She criticizes me*) on your map with body tension and uncover your requirements (*She shouldn't criticize me*). This skill of recognizing your requirements can change your entire life.

D. List all the requirements from your map:

_____

_____

_____

When you are not aware of your requirement (*My wife should not argue with me*), your I-System is kept active. You can only have intense cravings and be in an addicted mode when your I-System is active. The key to reducing cravings and managing your addiction is to be aware of your body tension and then recognize your requirement. This quiets your I-System, and your cravings settle down on their own.

2. Use the same situation from the previous map, and do a bridging map using your bridging awareness practices. Write the situation in the oval. Before you start writing, listen to any background sounds, feel your body's pressure on your seat, sense your feet on the floor, and feel the pen in your hand. Take your time. Once you feel settled, keep feeling the pen in your hand, and start writing. Watch the ink go onto the paper, and listen to any background sounds. Take a couple of minutes.

HIGH-RISK SITUATION MAP WITH BRIDGING

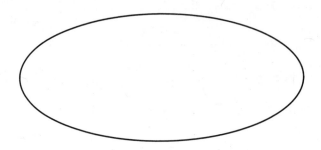

A. Is your mind cluttered or clear?

_____

B. Is your body tense or relaxed?

_____

C. In this mind-body state, how would you feel and act?

_____

D. What are the differences between the two maps?

_____

_____

You can do two-part maps whenever you have cravings and find yourself in an addicted mode. This will help you uncover the requirements that are creating your distress. When you quiet your I-System with your recovery tools, the grip of your addiction lessens. Mapping is a critical tool for you to heal from your addiction.

BEFRIEND YOUR BODY

1. Befriending your body is a mind-body bridging tool that is vital for managing your substance abuse. The location, type, amount, and buildup of body tension (such as chest pressure increasing) on the first High-Risk Situation map are clear-cut signals that when you have tension in that area of your body, your I-System is active. You are now in danger of experiencing amplified cravings and moving into an addicted mode.

   Like on the High-Risk Situation map, fill out the chart with other high-risk situations, and see if you can recognize the requirement embedded in each.

High-Risk Situation	Body Sensation	Behavior	Requirement
Money's short this week.	Tight chest, gets hard to breathe	Used	I shouldn't be short on money.
Walking past a bar	Stomach starts to churn	Stopped in front	I shouldn't have to walk past a bar.

2. Using your mind-body bridging tools, as you did on the High-Risk Situation Map with Bridging, you experienced a release of body tension. This is your natural state, your true self. Write down the same list of high-risk situations and use the mind-body bridging practices you have learned so far on each of the high-risk situations and then fill in the rest of the chart.

High-Risk Situation	Body Sensation	Behavior	Relapse Prevention Tool Applied
Money's short this week.	Breathing settles down	Less urge to use	Recognized my requirement "I shouldn't be short on money," labeled my thoughts.
Walking past a bar	Stomach settles	Kept on walking	Focusing on background sounds

Using your recovery tools throughout the day keeps you aware of your body's signals. It's important to notice the first signs of body tension, because when you don't, your body tension and discomfort can increase. Then your mind spins wildly with troubling thoughts until your body is all worked up and a full-blown craving occurs. It's critical that you recognize the early signs of body tension and troubling thoughts (addicted mode), and start using your recovery tools right away.

3. What recovery tools are working best for you? List them:

_____

_____

_____

TRIGGERS

Another important method of improving your ability to manage high-risk situations is to examine *triggers*. Each high-risk situation has one or several potential triggers. A *trigger* is a specific event or thought that activates a requirement, heating up your I-System. Any event or thought is a trigger if, and only if, that event or thought violates a requirement. Every coin has two sides, and even when flipped, it's still the same coin. Triggers and requirements are the same way. When you become aware of a trigger, it's important to realize that it's pointing you to the requirement (the other side of the coin). Remember, it's not the event, a thought, or someone else's behavior that activates the I-System; it's your requirement about that event, thought, or behavior.

Matthew was a thirty-six-year-old recovering cocaine addict. When he got home after work, he and his wife would often get into arguments. These arguments were more common when he had a stressful day at work, which would often lead him to experience intense emotional distress and cravings. He discussed this issue with his therapist, who suggested mind-body bridging techniques. Matthew began to realize that there were certain triggers that set him off when he came home to his wife. One of these triggers was his wife's tone of voice when she asked him to do something around the house. He saw that this triggered a requirement (*My wife should not use that tone of voice*). After realizing it was not his wife's tone of voice that upset him and made him angry but his unmet requirement about how she should talk, the arguments decreased. It shocked him to realize that small bits of his wife's behavior (tone of voice, critical gaze, use of words) had such a great impact on him. By recognizing his requirements for her behavior, they became closer than even before.

Life is full of events that upset you, make your I-System active, and create inner distress that drains your emotional resources. When you clearly recognize the triggers (events or thoughts) that switch on your I-System, they will not upset you as much as before. When someone's action toward you activates a very strong emotional response (for example, your wife is cold toward you), it helps to ask yourself, *What does that trigger behavior look like?* Some answers might be *Her loud voice*, and *The words she uses*. Next, look for your hidden requirements that go with each trigger action (*She shouldn't raise her voice* and *She should use kind words*).

Let's get up close and personal with your triggers. Take a few minutes to do a Triggers map by jotting down what triggers your I-System, such as the way others act or events that happen (for example, *Being bored, Going to social events, Feelings of self-pity*).

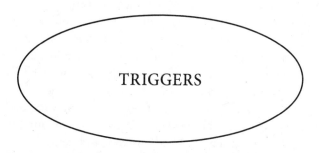

Choose the items from your map that are most likely to trigger cravings and activate your addicted mode. List these triggers, your associated body tension, and the underlying requirements. Mind-body mapping is always about your I-System requirements, not someone else's behavior. Remember that the trigger points to your requirement.

Trigger	Body Tension	Requirement
Being bored	Body feels restless	I should not be bored.
Going to a social event	Anxiety in stomach	I shouldn't feel anxious going to a social event.

USE YOUR BODY AS A COMPASS

Throughout the day, be aware of your body tension, especially those areas of your body that were tense on your Triggers map. Although the I-System lies at the root of your addicted mode, it's no more your enemy than a friend who is giving you vital information. Being aware of the early signs of body tension lets you know when you are heading in the wrong direction (toward an addicted mode). Use these signals as you would a compass (figure 2.1). When you notice that the I-System is on, know that you are off course. This is when you use your recovery tools to quiet your I-System, and your natural functioning will put you back on the right course.

Many times, your I-System's mind clutter keeps you from knowing how your body feels, and this sets the stage for cravings and your addicted mode. Many addicts are very disconnected from their bodies. They experience a certain type of numbness in their bodies. This state of "disembodiment" also contributes to being less aware of our feelings, a common feature of addiction. Becoming more attuned to bodily sensations helps you become aware of when you are in an addicted mode, and it builds "emotional intelligence." Becoming aware of bodily sensations will assist you and raise a red flag when you are about to enter into an addicted mode. The earlier you are aware of the process, the easier it will be to manage your addicted mode and to prevent relapse. Being aware of how your body responds is a crucial mind-body bridging tool. Use your body as a compass (befriend your body) to create mind-body balance in which you are in control of your life. Remember, when your body is tense and your mind cluttered, your I-System is in the driver's seat. To quiet your I-System, use your recovery tools by noting your body tension; recognizing that it's your requirement, not what's happening, that's causing your distress; and then listening to any background sounds, sensing whatever you're touching, and going back to your natural functioning. Remember, your I-System is your friend and there is no need to berate yourself whenever you notice an overactive I-System. That is your compass working. Gently return to using your recovery tools.

Headache   Muscle Aches

Tightness

Tension

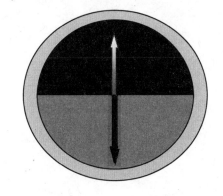

Clear Headed   Calm

Flexible   Relaxed

Figure 2.1 Use your body as a compass.

A bird that migrates has an inner compass that tells it when it's veering off course on its way home in the spring. When you notice your I-System in action, it becomes your compass, letting you know when you are off course. Being aware calms your I-System and shifts you into natural functioning. This puts you on course to deal with your daily life without the additional turmoil caused by your overactive I-System.

FINDING THE IMMEDIATE CAUSE OF YOUR CRAVINGS AND URGES

1. When your cravings and urges are triggered, and it's hard to find the underlying requirements, do a What's on My Mind map. Take a couple of minutes to write whatever pops into your mind around the following oval. Work quickly, without editing your thoughts.

WHAT'S ON MY MIND MAP

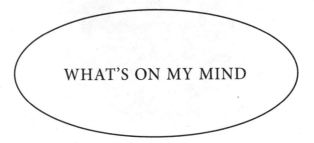

A. Is your mind cluttered or clear?

_____

B. Describe your body tension:

_____

_____

This is a momentary snapshot of what's on your mind. Notice which thoughts are connected to body tension (for example, *My daughter is acting out; I have to give a presentation; My car is too old*). Recognize the requirement in each thought (*My daughter shouldn't act out; I shouldn't have to give a presentation; I should have a new car*).

C. What are your requirements?

_____

_____

1. Do this map again, this time using your bridging awareness practices. Before you start writing, listen to any background sounds, feel your body's pressure on your seat, sense your feet on the floor, and feel the pen in your hand. Take your time. Once you feel settled, keep feeling the pen in your hand, and start writing. Watch the ink go onto the paper, and listen to any background sounds. For the next few minutes, jot down whatever thoughts pop into your mind.

WHAT'S ON MY MIND MAP WITH BRIDGING

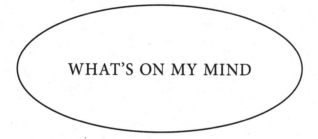

Observe the differences between the two maps:

_____

_____

_____

Remember, thought labeling helps. For example, if you have the thought *My life could be ruined*, say to yourself, *I'm having the thought, "My life could be ruined."* What is ruining your life right now isn't the difficult situation you're going through, but the thoughts your I-System has spun about this situation. You don't have to fix your thoughts, push them away, or force any changes. When the I-System is at rest, your true self in natural functioning will automatically help you make decisions about your course of action without the I-System clouding your mind. During the day, being aware that *a thought is just a thought* is all it takes; then you can return your awareness to the task at hand.

REVIEW

Discover

- That high-risk situations are problematic because your I-System is active.

- That your I-System prevents you from handling your cravings and urges.

- How your requirements activate your I-System.

- That quieting your I-System greatly reduces cravings and urges.

Experience

- Requirements are mental rules from your I-System that tell you how you and the world should be in each moment. When your I-System rules are broken, you become filled with body tension and troubling thoughts. You lose the ability to deal effectively with high-risk situations.

- Recognize requirements: When you become clearly aware that your requirement—not the events around you—is making your I-System active, you self-heal in a natural functioning state.

Apply

- To get in touch with and express your healing true self, use your mind-body bridging awareness practices every day. When you do, even a slight increase in jitteriness will remind you when to use your recovery tools, and you'll go back to being your true self.

- Recognizing requirements is an essential skill in managing your addiction. When you begin to recognize your requirements that trigger your cravings, which activate your addicted mode, you will develop the skills to live a life as your true self, not dominated by your I-System. Mind-body bridging is an ongoing practice. Use your recovery tools to live every aspect of your life with a calm I-System. Your new recovery tools from this chapter are listed below.

Recovery Tools

➢ Create two-part mind-body maps whenever you begin to feel yourself moving into an addicted mode. A map a day helps to keep the cravings at bay.

➢ Discover how requirements activate your I-System.

➢ Recognize requirements to quiet your I-System.

➢ Use your body as a compass by befriending your body.

MBB RATING SCALE: DEAL EFFECTIVELY WITH HIGH-RISK SITUATIONS

Date: _____

After using the tools in this chapter for several days, check the description that best matches your practice for each question: hardly ever, sometimes, usually, or almost always.

How often do you...	Hardly Ever	Sometimes	Usually	Almost Always
Locate and recognize body tension as a sign of an overactive I-System?				
Notice the destructive effects that the I-System has upon your life?				
Notice that an overactive I-System is underlying your anxiety?				
Recognize your requirements?				
Catch yourself drifting away from being present in the moment?				
Use bridging awareness practices to quiet the I-System and improve the quality of your life?				
Come to appreciate your life in a different light?				
Do a daily two-part mind-body map?				

When your I-System is active, how do you deal with your anxiety?

_____

_____

When you are using your anxiety reduction tools and your I-System is quiet, how do you deal with difficult situations?

_____

_____

What's the most important benefit of doing two-part mind-body maps?

_____

CHAPTER 3

MANAGE NEGATIVE THINKING AND HEAL TOXIC SHAME

Discover, Experience, and Apply

Discover how your depressor stops you from managing your negative thoughts and sets the stage for substance abuse.

Experience how taking charge of your depressor helps you manage your troubling thoughts and allows you to continue self-healing your addiction.

Apply your recovery tools in your daily life.

Mind-Body Language

Depressor: A part of the I-System that takes your natural negative thoughts and self-talk (things you say to yourself) and creates body tension and mind clutter. It constitutes a major part of your habitual addictive thinking patterns. It makes you feel weak, powerless, and vulnerable, and it fuels your addicted mode.

Storyline: Thoughts that your I-System spins into stories (true or not) that sustain your I-System and substance abuse, and pull you away from what you are presently doing.

Defusing the depressor: When you become clearly aware that your negative thoughts are "just thoughts," you reduce the power of the depressor. This allows your mind-body to start healing from your addiction.

THE CAUSE OF YOUR DESTRUCTIVE NEGATIVE THINKING

Your mind works in opposites. If you have the thought *high*, there must be a *low*; if you think *good*, there must be a *bad*; and the same follows for *happy* and *sad*, *calm* and *angry*, *sick* and *well*, and *young* and *old*. The mind works with both positive and negative thoughts. Most of us struggle over what to do with our negative thoughts. The issue is not negative thoughts as such, but rather when the I-System captures those negative thoughts. Negative thoughts captured by the I-System are one of the central components of habitual thought patterns that sustain your addicted mode. I-System-captured negative thinking, often associated with addiction, consists of excessive thoughts of fear, anger, self-doubt, resentment, self-pity, blame, and so forth. Your addicted mode is fortified by a complex network of negative thoughts that justifies and sustains your substance abuse.

Many people try to use positive affirmations to get rid of or deal with their negative thoughts. We have all tried to fix ourselves with positive affirmations, but when we stop, the negative thoughts come back with a vengeance. So what do we do about negative thoughts? Have you noticed that pushing them away only gives them more energy? For example, try not to think of a red balloon. What are you thinking of? A red balloon! The only time we will get rid of our negative thoughts is when we're brain-dead.

So the question remains: What do we do with negative thoughts? The answer is not so much related to *what* to do, but rather *who* is thinking the negative thought—your damaged self, driven by your I-System, or your natural true self. For instance, happiness and sadness are emotions that we all have. Your true self knows how to deal with these emotions. But the I-System's damaged self has a much different approach. Its mission is to keep itself switched on by grabbing thoughts, usually negative ones. The *depressor*, a part of the I-System, works by taking your negative thoughts and self-talk and creating body tension and mind clutter that result in a painful and distressing experience. It takes a negative thought like *I'm a loser*, *I can't cope*, or *I'm no good* and weaves a story about that thought, filling every cell of your body with negativity. You see yourself as powerless, broken, or ruined, and you have a story and a body full of tension and misery to prove it!

THE DEPRESSOR AND TOXIC SHAME

Recovery experts like John Bradshaw (1988) point out that at the core of addiction is toxic shame. A shame-based belief system is essentially composed of negative thoughts about yourself, captured by your depressor, which you believe to be true. Such a belief system results in a mind-body state known as the *damaged self*. This damaged self is experienced as toxic shame, which makes you feel that you are fundamentally flawed, and that you need to be *fixed*. I-System-induced shame drives substance abuse in a futile effort to repair this illusion of the damaged self.

Shame-based thinking precedes and follows a relapse. The depressor is very active after a relapse, and therefore tills the soil for future relapse. It becomes a vicious cycle, where after each relapse there are more powerful negative depressor thoughts and body sensations, which in turn make you more prone to subsequent relapse. Your damaged self uses the depressor to keep itself in control. It is not the contents of your negative thoughts that lead to toxic shame, but rather the activity of your depressor.

The mental and physical distress caused by the I-System's depressor is one of the main reasons for not self-healing your addiction, so it's very important to be clearly aware of your negative thoughts and feelings about yourself. It's important for you to see how the I-System's depressor perpetuates the negative thinking that keeps your addicted mode in operation. The original question *What do I do about my negative thoughts?* now becomes *What do I do about my depressor?* The depressor is the doom and gloom of your I-System and damaged self. It uses the negative self-talk that naturally occurs during the day to make you feel weak and powerless. Today you'll begin to see your negative self-talk for what it is—just thoughts. This is another crucial step in your becoming able to stay in your natural functioning and avoid relapse.

Try hard to recall your negative self-talk from the past twenty-four hours. On this chart, note your thoughts, the kind of body tension you have, and where it's located. Notice how the intensity of your negative thoughts is related to your level of body tension.

Negative Self-Talk	Body Tension
I'm not a good person, nothing I do is good enough, I'll give up trying.	*Sweating, building pressure in chest, and its getting harder to breathe*

Recognizing your negative self-talk may not, at first, seem to be directly related to your specific anxiety symptoms. Some people have even said that their negative self-talk is due to their inability to cope and control their addiction. But what we have discovered is that when your depressor is in control of your negative thoughts, it will continue to create so much mental and physical chaos that your addicted mode keeps growing. The secret to preventing your negative thinking from fueling your addiction is to know how the depressor works, how it fills your body with unpleasant feelings, and how it stops you from self-healing. The next maps will give you more tools to unlock the healing ability of your powerful self.

DISCOVER HOW THE DEPRESSOR STOPS YOU FROM MANAGING YOUR NEGATIVE THINKING

1. Do a Depressor map. Around the oval, write any negative thoughts and self-talk you have when you're disappointed with yourself or bummed out. If any of the thoughts are positive, see if you can find their negative opposites and jot them down (see the sample map on the next page). Write as much as you can for a couple of minutes.

DEPRESSOR MAP

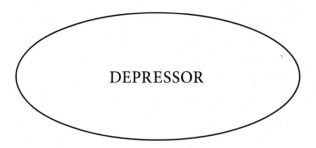

DEPRESSOR

A. Describe your body tension and how it progresses:

_____

B. What's your behavior like when your depressor is active?

_____

_____

C. Describe the impact on your addiction and quality of life when your depressor is active:

_____

The thoughts on your map are natural thoughts that happen to be negative. The depressor works by grabbing a natural negative thought and embedding the negativity in your body. This process creates a heavy mental and physical burden that prevents healing and reinforces your addiction.

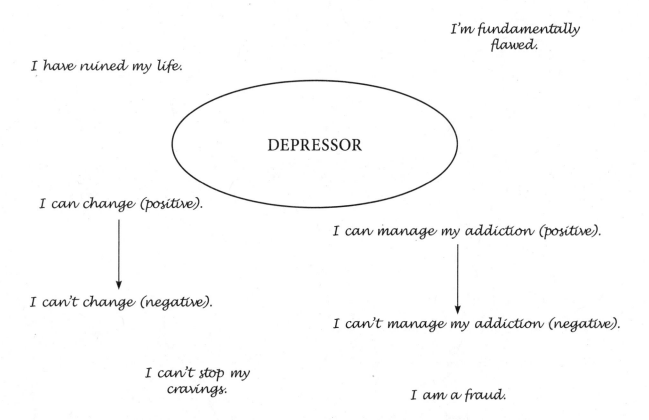

SAMPLE MAP: DEPRESSOR

I'm bad.

My family doesn't support me.

I'm a loser.

I'm fundamentally flawed.

I have ruined my life.

DEPRESSOR

I can change (positive).

I can manage my addiction (positive).

I can't change (negative).

I can't manage my addiction (negative).

I can't stop my cravings.

I am a fraud.

A. Describe your body tension and how it progresses: *Tight shoulders, heavy body. The more negative my thoughts, the more my shoulders rise and the heavier my body feels.*

B. What's your behavior like when your depressor is active? *I first keep to myself, and then the worrying thoughts overwhelm me and I end up not being able to do anything.*

2. Time to look at your depressor more closely. From your previous Depressor map, take the thought that troubles you the most by creating a lot of body tension (for example, *I can't stop my cravings*), and write it in the following oval. Now, for the next few minutes, write around the oval any thoughts that come to mind. Use phrases or complete sentences like *Nothing I do works, Why me?* or *It's hopeless; I will die an addict.*

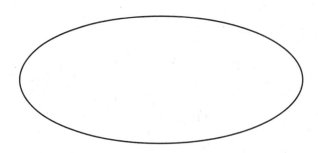

TROUBLING THOUGHT FROM MY DEPRESSOR MAP

Describe your body tension and how it progresses:

_____

_____

The map you just did holds the key to managing your depressor. The thoughts on your map are spun into stories (true or not) by your I-System. Think about the stories that come to mind about your negative thoughts and addiction. These are called *storylines*. It's very important to recognize and become aware of how they control you. Storylines are the link between the negative thoughts that pop into your mind and the mind-body distress you experienced on your last two maps. The I-System's spinning storyline takes a natural negative thought and embeds the negativity into every cell of your body. Storylines keep the I-System going, taking you away from the present moment. Stopping the depressor's storylines keeps negative thoughts from creating a painful mind-body state that drives your addiction.

BEGIN TO EXPERIENCE HOW TO MANAGE YOUR NEGATIVE THINKING

Using your bridging awareness practices, do the previous map again. Write the same troubling thought in the oval. Before you continue, listen to background sounds, feel your body's pressure on your seat, sense your feet on the floor, and feel the pen in your hand. Take your time. Once you feel settled, keep feeling the pen in your hand and start writing. Watch the ink go onto the paper, and listen to background sounds. Write for a couple of minutes.

TROUBLING THOUGHT FROM MY DEPRESSOR MAP WITH BRIDGING

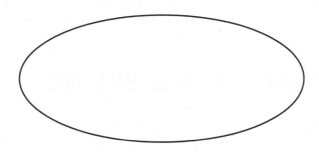

Notice the differences between the two maps:

A. Is your mind cluttered or clear?

_____

B. Is your body tense or relaxed?

_____

C. In this mind-body state, how do you act?

_____

What is at stake here is not learning how to manage your symptoms of addiction, but eliminating the root cause of your addicted mode—the activity of your depressor.

STEPS TO DEFUSE YOUR DEPRESSOR AND CONTINUE SELF-HEALING

When you feel weighed down by your negative troubling thoughts and have body tension, your depressor is active. Use the tools below to defuse your depressor and let your true self get back in the driver's seat:

1. *Recognizing the depressor:* When you observe that your mind has negative thoughts and your body has tension, know it's your depressor—not the thoughts, what's happening, or other people—that is causing your distress.

2. *Thought labeling:* Thought labeling is the first tool you use to control your troubling thoughts. From one of your maps, choose a thought that still creates body tension. Say slowly to yourself, *I am having the thought* _____ [insert your thought]. Are you sensing a reduction of body tension? Remember, it's your depressor, not the content of your thoughts, that causes your distress.

3. *Bridging awareness practices:* If you still feel body tension after using the steps above, listen to background sounds, and feel your behind on the chair and your feet on the floor. Do you experience less body tension? If so, you are defusing your depressor.

STORYLINE AWARENESS BREAKS YOUR DENIAL

Another powerful tool for managing your addicted mode is storyline awareness. Remember, storylines are thoughts spun into stories that keep your I-System's damaged self and addicted mode active. Storylines aren't just stories; they have a harmful physical effect on your body and cloud your mind. The negative storylines tend to define us, and the positive ones tend to confine us.

The self-defeating image you have of yourself, is stored in your mind and body; *mind-body representational world*. The mind-body representational world is a mental picture you have of yourself and the world, and interacts with all the systems of your body. Your storylines create a negative self-image and a painful, tense, poorly regulated body. As this happens, the mind-body representational world generates more requirements of how you and the world should be. When these new requirements are violated the I-System is reactivated, causing your depressor to generate more storylines to further adversely influence your mind-body world and strengthen your urges and cravings.

All storylines keep you living in the past or dreaming of the future. This takes you away from being present in the moment and handling what's happening right now with your true self in charge. Storyline awareness is simply noticing the storyline, seeing the damage it's doing, and letting your awareness stop the story. Your natural functioning is restored without your even trying.

Each addict has extensive storylines that sustain their addiction. For recovery, it is imperative to be aware of the storylines that fuel your addiction. These storylines that fuel your addiction can only come into being when your I-System is active.

Joe, who grew up in an emotionally unstable home, was referred to mind-body bridging by his doctor for his eating disorder and colitis. As a child, he had become so anxious over his family situation that he had developed colitis and couldn't speak or eat in front of other people. Over time he began using, thinking it would reduce his anxiety. Through mind-body bridging, he learned how to label his troubling thoughts and used the bridging awareness practices to get through his day. Using additional recovery tools, he became aware of his requirements and his storylines about himself, his family (especially his father), and growing up in a volatile home. He learned that his depressor used memories about his angry, bitter father (who took every opportunity to ridicule him) and his passive, anxious mother (who didn't stand up for him) to create current storylines that were keeping him trapped in an addicted mode. Joe began to see that these storylines were trapping him. As he continued to recognize his requirements and storylines, Joe's childhood became a past memory. He now knows that memories are just thoughts, and *a thought is just a thought*. Joe is living his life in the present moment without being troubled by substance abuse or colitis.

By using your storyline awareness tool (just being aware of the storyline) during the day, you'll see how much of your time storylines swallow up. You don't need to push the story away; you just need to become aware of it and know that this is I-System driven. Your awareness dissolves the storyline and will even help you sleep better at night. Your addicted mode cannot exist without extensive storylines, in the same way that fungi need dark and damp environments to grow in. By shining the light of your awareness on I-System storylines, you take away the fuel of your addicted mode.

Alwin has tried many times to achieve a sustainable recovery. He often stays clean for six months at a time but eventually relapses, even though he is actively engaged in many recovery practices. Alwin's periods of sobriety and subsequent relapses follow a pattern: as soon as his life begins to stabilize, he is plagued by constant self-doubt and negative self-talk, such as *I have wasted so much of my life; I am hopeless; I am a loser; I will never be successful at anything; My life is boring and empty*. A colleague at work recommended mind-body bridging. After learning the bridging awareness and thought labeling tools, whenever a negative thought would pop up, Alwin would label that thought, come to his senses, and return to what he was doing. Alwin learned about his I-System's depressor and how it captures natural negative thoughts and embeds the negativity in his body. Alwin began doing depressor maps and learned how his I-System was making him feel victimized and weak, and what role it played in his relapses. His outlook began to change as he mapped daily and used his recovery tools whenever he recognized that his I-System was active. Now, when a negative thought pops up, after he labels this thought as just a thought, he adds a lighthearted *So what else is new?* and goes about his day. He is now over two years clean.

Think back to situations over the past week, where your I-System created negative storylines that led to your addicted mode. Note the body tension that came with the situation, and find your hidden requirement.

Fill out the chart below:

Situation	Negative Storylines	Body Tension	Requirement
Starting a new job	I know I will get fired eventually; if I get fired I might as well use again.	Start sweating, feel heart beating harder	I should be good at my new job. My recovery depends on me staying employed.
She criticized me.	I'll never be good enough for her.	Band around my head, jaw tight, grinding my teeth	Now that I am in recovery, she should not criticize me.

Start mulling over one of your most distressing storylines and try to keep it going. Now, become aware of background sounds. While continuing to listen to the sounds, observe how your storyline unfolds. Is the storyline running out of gas? Using your bridging awareness practices weakens your storylines. If you still have a troubling thought (*I will get fired*), label the thought (*I'm having the thought, "I will get fired"*) and realize that it's not the possibility of getting fired but the thought that is causing your distress. Once a thought is captured by the I-System, you're prevented from dealing with that thought or situation in a healthy way. When you realize a thought is just a thought and a story is just a story, the thought will not activate your I-System. You will be free to deal with all of your thoughts with your true self in charge.

MANAGE YOUR "WHAT IFS"

1. The following maps take a look at those "what ifs" that create excessive anxiety whenever you think about them or even try not to think about them. Do a What If map. Take a couple of minutes to write around the oval any "what if" thoughts that come to mind about important situations in your life that may have a negative outcome (see the sample map on the following page). Work quickly, without editing your thoughts.

WHAT IF MAP

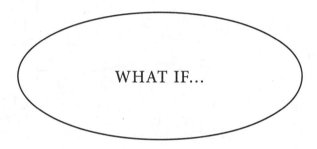

A. Describe your initial body tension and how it progresses to anxiety:

_____

_____

B. List your depressors and storylines:

_____

_____

C. List your requirements:

_____

_____

D. In this mind-body state, how do you act?

_____

SAMPLE MAP: WHAT IF

...my children have
addiction problems?

...I lose my job?

...I relapse?

...I have cravings the
rest of my life?

...recovery is boring?

WHAT IF...

...my mother doesn't
recover from surgery?

...I'm gone, what will happen to the kids?

...I never find a job?

...this workbook
doesn't help me?

A. Describe your body tension and how it progresses: *Started with a knot in my stomach, but the more I go over the "what ifs," the more my whole body tenses up and I end up urgently needing to go to the bathroom.*

2. Use your bridging awareness practices and do the map again. Before you begin to write, listen to background sounds, feel your body's pressure on your seat, sense your feet on the floor, and feel the pen in your hand. Take your time. Once you feel settled, keep feeling the pen in your hand and start writing. Watch the ink go onto the paper, and listen to background sounds. Write for a couple of minutes.

WHAT IF MAP WITH BRIDGING

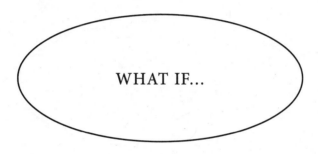

Notice the differences between the two maps:

A. Is your mind cluttered or clear?

_____

B. Is your body tense or relaxed?

_____

C. In this mind-body state, how do you act?

_____

_____

D. Are you more likely to successfully heal your addiction in this mind-body state than on the previous map?   Yes _____   No _____

RESOLVE YOUR RESERVATIONS

1. Apart from the "what ifs" that lead to excessive anxiety, recovering addicts often have one or many "what ifs" called reservations, in the form of *If _____, then I will use.* Reservations are certain situations that we reserve for using: for instance, *If my wife leaves me, then I will use; If I get cancer, I will use.* Write the reservation that causes you the most worry in the oval. Next, take a couple of minutes to write around the oval any additional thoughts (storylines) that come to mind. Work quickly, without editing your thoughts.

RESERVATIONS MAP

A. Describe your body tension and how it progresses:

_____

_____

B. List your depressors and storylines:

_____

_____

C. List your requirements (Item: *If my wife leaves I will use;* Requirement: *My wife shouldn't leave*):

_____

_____

The reason your reservation (*If my wife leaves I will use*) is damaging to you is because the embedded requirement (*My wife shouldn't leave*) causes an impaired mind-body state (damaged self) when you even think about the possibility of her leaving. That impaired mind-body state is damaging your relationship here and now. Even if she leaves, isn't it better to deal with that eventuality with your true self being disappointed rather than your damaged self being devastated?

2. Using your bridging awareness practices, do the previous map again. Write the same reservation in the oval. Before you continue, listen to background sounds, feel your body's pressure on your seat, sense your feet on the floor, and feel the pen in your hand. Take your time. Once you feel settled, keep feeling the pen in your hand and start writing. Watch the ink go onto the paper, and listen to background sounds. Write for a couple of minutes.

RESERVATIONS MAP WITH BRIDGING

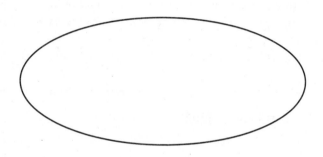

Notice the differences between the two maps:

A. Is your mind cluttered or clear?

_____

B. Is your body tense or relaxed?

_____

C. In this mind-body state, how likely are you to have reservations?

_____

QUESTIONS TO PUT YOU IN CHARGE OF YOUR NEGATIVE THOUGHTS

Answer the following questions when your troubling thoughts are getting you down:

1. What are the signals that your depressor is active (*heavy body, knot in stomach, "I'm not good enough" thoughts, feelings of self-pity*)?

   _____

2. What is your behavior like when your depressor gets you down (*overeat, use drugs, isolate*)?

   _____

   _____

3. How is the depressor getting in the way of your executive functioning (*I'm not making good decisions, my parenting is inconsistent, I often relapse, I feel a lot of pressure to fix how I feel*)?

   _____

   _____

4. Do you experience yourself as losing control of your life?   Yes _____   No _____
   How so?

   _____

5. What are your storylines (*I'll never be able to stop using; My addiction is because of what I went through*)?

   _____

   _____

6. Are these thoughts and storylines creating who you are?   Yes _____   No _____
   How so?

   _____

7. What are your requirements (*I shouldn't be an addict; Recovery should be easy*)?

   _____

   _____

Be aware that it's not the content or accuracy of your negative thoughts or stories that are behind your addicted mode; it's the activity of your depressor. Use your recovery tools of bridging awareness practices, thought labeling, storyline awareness, and recognition of requirements to self-heal your addiction.

REVIEW

Discover

- How your depressor stops you from managing your negative thoughts and sets the stage for substance abuse.

- How defusing the depressor puts you in charge of your troubling thoughts and allows you to continue self-healing your addiction.

Experience

- Your depressor makes you feel weak, powerless, and vulnerable, and it sets the stage for your addicted mode. It is a part of the I-System that takes your natural negative thoughts and self-talk (things you say to yourself) and creates body tension and mind clutter. It constitutes a major part of your habitual addictive thinking patterns.

- Your storylines are thoughts that your I-System spins into stories (true or not). These sustain your I-System and substance abuse, and pull you away from living your best life.

- When you defuse your depressor, you become clearly aware that your negative thoughts are "just thoughts." By reducing the power of the depressor, your mind-body automatically begins healing from your addiction.

Apply

Mark was a psychology student who had been in recovery for three years for his substance abuse. After he cleaned up, he began suffering from major depressive episodes. In these depressive episodes, Mark was plagued by extreme self-doubt and fear about his future. He constantly worried about getting good grades and what would happen if he failed to get his degree. He struggled to sleep and to focus on his studies. Mark finally sought help and his therapist recommended mind-body bridging practices. He began to see clearly how the depressor created body tension when it grabbed onto thoughts like *I will never pass my final exam,* and *I'm not smart enough.* Mark learned to use thought labeling to keep his negative thoughts from creating mind clutter and unpleasant body tension. He acknowledged that his storylines took up most of his day and prevented him from focusing on his studies and healthy recovery practices. Mapping helped him recognize his requirements about his future and getting good grades. Using all of his recovery tools, Mark was able to make better decisions and focus on his studies, and his depression episodes became less frequent and less severe.

Let's look at the recovery tools Mark used.

1. He used his bridging awareness tools to calm his I-System and gain access to his innate self-healing powers.

2. He recognized it was his depressor—not his negative thoughts—that was making him feel bad.

3. He used thought labeling to get control of his troubling thoughts.

4. He became aware that the spin of his storylines pulled him away from the present moment.

5. He was able to recognize his requirements, shift into a natural functioning state, and succeed in college.

Below are the three new tools discussed in this chapter. Use them with the tools you learned in the previous two chapters to defuse your depressor, access your powerful self, and continue to self-heal from your addiction.

Recovery Tools

➢ Recognize the depressor's activity.

➢ Become aware of your storyline.

➢ Defuse the depressor.

MBB RATING SCALE: MANAGE NEGATIVE THINKING AND HEAL TOXIC SHAME

Date: _____

After using the tools in this chapter for several days, check the description that best matches your practice: hardly ever, sometimes, usually, or almost always.

How often do you...	Hardly Ever	Sometimes	Usually	Almost Always
Notice negative self-talk and body tension as a sign of the depressor?				
Notice that your depressor is running wild and making you feel weak and powerless?				
Experience that the damaged self comes from your I-System?				
Recognize that an active depressor sets the stage for anxiety attacks?				
Defuse your depressor by staying aware of what it is doing and using thought labeling?				
Recognize storylines?				
Recognize your self-healing power when your I-System is quiet?				

List the body tension that comes along with the depressor and how it progresses:

_____

List the themes of two storylines:

_____

_____

List two behaviors that are connected with the depressor:

_____

_____

What's it like to defuse your depressor and live with a quiet I-System?

_____

CHAPTER 4

WHY YOUR BEST EFFORTS SEEM TO GO WRONG

Discover, Experience, and Apply

Discover how your fixer drives your substance abuse and daily activities.

Experience how defusing the fixer helps you overcome your addiction.

Apply your recovery tools in your daily life.

Mind-Body Language

Fixer: The depressor's partner that drives your substance abuse and daily activities with overactive, never-ending thoughts of how to fix yourself and the world.

Defusing the fixer: When you become clearly aware (at the time you are doing something) that your fixer is active and use your recovery tools, you take away the fixer's power. Right away, you feel a shift from a stressful, addicted mode to one with a ready and relaxed mind and body. You can now calmly take care of yourself and whatever you have to do in natural functioning.

Depressor/fixer cycle: These I-System partners create a vicious cycle, keeping the I-System going and sustaining your addiction.

WHEN ENOUGH IS NEVER ENOUGH

You now know that at the root of your painful toxic shame and your addicted mode is the depressor. The depressor creates a mind-body state, the damaged self, which is so unbearable that you have to do something to change it. This is where the fixer comes into play. The *fixer* is a component of the I-System that tries to fix the painful, damaged mind-body state that the depressor creates. From a mind-body bridging perspective, substance abuse or any addiction is understood as an attempt to "fix" the pain associated with the damaged self. All addictive behavior is fixer-driven. It is no coincidence that using drugs is often referred to as having a "fix."

Requirements, depressors, and fixers are the three major parts of the I-System. Requirements are the I-System's rules about how you and the world should be. When a requirement is broken, this switches on the I-System. Then the depressor and fixer jump in, interact with each other, and keep the I-System going. The fixer is the depressor's lifelong, faithful partner that drives you unsuccessfully to repair the painful shame-based state the depressor has caused. The fixer starts from the false belief (caused by the depressor) that you are damaged, tries to fix you, and works by making you believe it's really helping you. A central component of the addicted mode is that your choices become limited to certain predictable and habitual behaviors, over which you feel powerless. For example, you tell yourself that you will never take drugs again, and you feel convinced that you will be able to stick to your decision. Then it is as if a switch is flipped on: your I-System is activated, and now in your addicted mode using seems like a good idea, you have storylines that back it up, and you score and use.

The fixer can also have a positive appearance: refusing that extra cookie, exercising today, spending more time with family and loved ones, having fun, procrastinating less, working a good recovery program, staying relaxed, feeling less stress, being better disciplined, making better decisions, finding the right career, and landing the perfect job. How successful have you been? Were they just this year's batch of New Year's resolutions? Were you confident that if you could fix yourself, you would have less stress and a better life? Even if you achieved a fixer goal, did you ever have peace of mind and a sense of well-being?

In this chapter, you'll discover the main reason your attempts have either failed or not seemed good enough, even when you reached a goal. The fixer's job is to make you *think* it is helping you by pushing you to "try harder" and "be stronger" while filling you with body tension. Your fixer comes up with never-ending thoughts and storylines that focus on how to fix you and the world. It brings a sense of urgency and pressure to your activities, and when it's in play, enough is never going to be enough. The fixer starts from the false belief that you are broken, tries to fix you, and works by making you believe it's really helping you. You can recognize the fixer by noticing your increased body tension and a mind full of thoughts like *Try harder, Do more, Be smarter,* or *Be stronger.* No matter what you accomplish, the depressor jumps in with thoughts like *not good enough,* further activating your fixer. The depressor and fixer work together in a depressor/fixer cycle, keeping the I-System going and leading to the disruptive mind-body state of the damaged self. Whether the fixer is driving your substance use or daily activities, it has the same aim. As long as your depressor is making you feel damaged, your fixer is going to attempt to fix you. The energy and commotion of the depressor/fixer cycle is the sole moving force of your addiction.

MEET YOUR FIXER

1. In this mapping exercise, jot down around the oval the thoughts that come up about "How I Am Going to Improve My Life." Work quickly for a couple of minutes, without editing your thoughts.

HOW I AM GOING TO IMPROVE MY LIFE MAP

HOW I AM GOING TO
IMPROVE MY LIFE

A. Looking at your overall map, how do you feel?

Calm _____   Tense _____   Overwhelmed _____

B. Consider each item on your map and figure out how much body tension you have when you think about going for this self-improvement goal. Next to each item on your map, note your level of body tension using one of these symbols: Ø for no body tension, + for mild, ++ for moderate, or +++ for severe. It may help to see the sample map at the end of the exercise.

The statements on your map may be either fixer thoughts from an active I-System or natural thoughts. The thoughts that come with body tension are fixer thoughts from your I-System (damaged self), and the thoughts with no body tension are from natural functioning (true self). Your challenge is telling the difference between the two. Body tension that comes with thoughts means your I-System is active. The fixer brings a mental urgency, creating extra pressure for you to act. Remember, natural functioning is how you think, feel, see the world, and act when your I-System is quiet. When you are in natural functioning and don't reach a goal, you're naturally disappointed. But when you don't reach a fixer goal, you feel devastated; your mind spins with negative thoughts, and your body is tense. For all your efforts and good intentions to succeed, it's important to know which of your daily activities the fixer is capturing.

C. Again, look over each item on your map and imagine that you're not going to reach that goal. Describe what happens to your body tension. Note how you feel:

_____

_____

D. If you now have body tension and mind clutter for items that were previously at level Ø, those items have become fixer thoughts. List your fixer thoughts from this map:

_____

_____

_____

E. List your thoughts on this map that are from executive functioning (tension-free):

_____

_____

2. It's important to compare the Depressor map in chapter 3 (the first map in that chapter) to this Fixer map titled "How I Am Going to Improve My Life":

A. Which map has the higher overall energy levels (makes you feel better)?

Depressor map _____   Fixer map _____

The higher levels of energy that may come with the fixer and make you believe that you feel better aren't unusual. This higher endorphin level can keep you from recognizing your fixer, because you feel good about the thoughts. When active, the fixer clouds your judgment and affects your actions.

B. Your body is always giving you helpful information. Note the differences in location, quality, and intensity of the body tension that comes with the thoughts on the Depressor and Fixer maps (for example, *My body tension on the Depressor map was located around my gut, and my body felt heavy and unresponsive; on my Fixer map, my body tension is around my chest and head, and there's a jittery feeling*).

_____

_____

The intensity of your body tension and the driving pressure of your storylines are important signs that your I-System's fixer is active. Storylines are a sign that your fixer is restricting your ability to deal effectively with your current situation.

SAMPLE MAP: HOW I AM GOING TO IMPROVE MY LIFE

Control my using ++

Find a new job ++

*Repair my damaged
relationships +++*

Be a better parent ++

Begin meditating +

HOW I AM GOING TO
IMPROVE MY LIFE

Get a degree +++

*Work a good recovery
program +++*

Wash my car Ø

Be more spiritual +++

Fixer thoughts come with body tension when you think about trying to reach your goals or imagine that you won't reach your goals (for example, *Be a better parent, Work a good recovery program, Get a degree*). Also note any thoughts from natural functioning (without body tension, marked Ø) (for example, *Wash my car*).

THE MASKS OF THE FIXER

The mask of the fixer takes many forms. For instance, Mike is driven to work a 60-hour week. Kader has shoulder injuries from excessive workouts in the gym. Joan suffers chronic exhaustion from taking too many courses for her degree. Tom drinks a six-pack every night to calm down after work. Kim avoids so many activities and places that her life is very limited.

The fixer will mask itself as the great savior in your life. At first the fixer may seem to improve your life. Remember, the fixer's real job is to fix how the depressor makes you feel—ashamed and damaged— and to keep the I-System going. At times, the fixer uses thoughts like *I need to get a better job, I have to find a loving relationship, I need to get a degree, I need to control my using*, or *I have to get rich*, which hide the underlying depressor thoughts: *I'm useless, I'm unlovable, I'm stupid*, or *I am nothing without money*. These hidden depressor thoughts make you feel so awful that your fixer drives you relentlessly to do something.

The fixer activates mental pressure, stirs up your body, and urges you to act. It drives your actions and fills you with a feeling of urgency. Be aware of the way your fixer frames the demand. The fixer traps you into thinking, *I need to, I have to, I must*, or *I will*. When your I-System is switched on and the fixer is in the driver's seat, it can relentlessly drive you toward perfectionism and unattainable goals. The fixer pushes you to do things that are apparently aimed at improving your life, but end up further limiting your life. Notice the fixer's early signs of body tension, storylines, and mental pressure.

Never underestimate the urgency the fixer creates when it tries to fix your shame-based, damaged self. Since these fixer thoughts come with mental and physical pressure, they drive fixer activities in a failed attempt to fix how your depressor makes you feel. The depressor's main task is to make you feel damaged and not good enough, and perpetuate your toxic shame. However, after you do the fixer-driven activity, your depressor creates more negative feelings, and this pushes the fixer back into action. This creates a stressful, vicious cycle (depressor/fixer/depressor/fixer…). All of this builds so much tension and mental turmoil that it solidifies toxic shame, leading to relapse.

The truth is that no amount of fixer action or fixer-driven success can change internalized toxic shame. This shame, caused by your I-System, is an illusion. No amount of fixing can fix an illusion. The depressor causes a mind-body wound that the fixer cannot heal. Even fixer activity that seems adaptive, like working harder or apologizing, will not heal this wound. For instance, you might think that if you become wealthy, your feelings of shame and brokenness will disappear. Wealth or even abstinence will not "fix" your feelings of shame and of being broken. Even when your attempts seem positive, your successes don't often last very long because they are driven by your I-System. To break this cycle, become actively aware of the fixer's mental and physical pressure that drives your activity, and recognize your depressor, which lies beneath the surface.

YOUR FIXER HAS AN UNDERLYING DEPRESSOR

1. Every fixer has an embedded depressor that drives it. Look again at the fixer map, "How I Am Going to Improve My Life." Write down your embedded depressor thoughts under the fixer thoughts. See the following sample map.

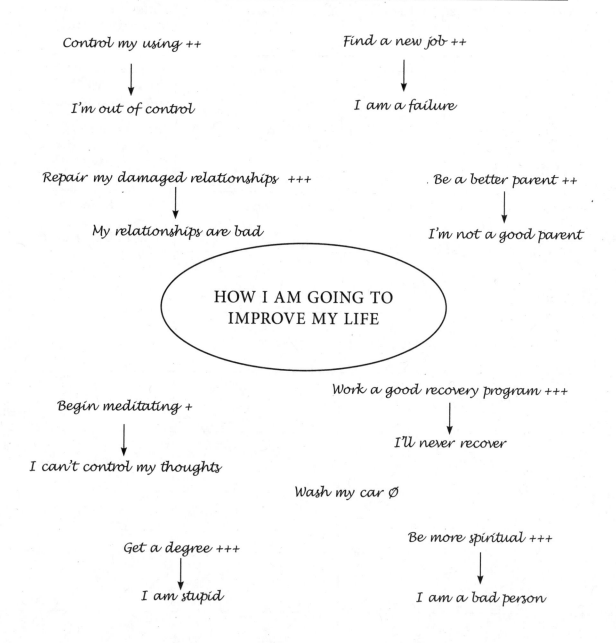

SAMPLE MAP: HOW I AM GOING TO IMPROVE MY LIFE
WITH DEPRESSOR THOUGHTS

Control my using ++
↓
I'm out of control

Find a new job ++
↓
I am a failure

Repair my damaged relationships +++
↓
My relationships are bad

Be a better parent ++
↓
I'm not a good parent

HOW I AM GOING TO
IMPROVE MY LIFE

Begin meditating +
↓
I can't control my thoughts

Work a good recovery program +++
↓
I'll never recover

Wash my car Ø

Get a degree +++
↓
I am stupid

Be more spiritual +++
↓
I am a bad person

2. Think about last weekend. The fixer is always active when you attempt to escape from how the depressor makes you feel. Below, note any of your activities that created mental or physical pressure (fixer activity). Can you find the embedded depressor activity? Note your body tension with Ø for none, + for mild, ++ for moderate, or +++ for severe.

Fixer-Driven Behavior	Tension Level	Depressor Thoughts	Storyline
Watched TV for most of the weekend.	++	I am useless.	Nothing I do will be successful.
Searched the internet for many hours for a new self-help book.	+++	I'm damaged.	I must find a way to improve myself.
Isolated myself.	+++	I am boring.	Now that I don't drink, I won't be interesting to others.
Spent the weekend sharpening and cleaning tools.	++	My tools are not right.	Tools have to be perfect, so I have to find every dull, dirty edge.
Binged on ice cream.	+++	I am alone.	I don't have any friends, because I have nothing to offer.

A. When your fixer was active, what were the outcomes of your behavior? For example, *Binged on ice cream: felt bloated and ashamed, and felt even more isolated.*

_____

_____

_____

_____

B. When you had depressor thoughts, how did you feel?

_____

_____

C. Did your fixer jump in to fix the depressor thoughts?   Yes _____   No _____

D. How did your storylines keep the depressor/fixer cycle going?

_____

_____

_____

_____

E. What were the hidden requirements you were trying to meet (*My home should be perfect, My garage should be in order, I should not be bored, I should not have discouraging thoughts*)?

_____

_____

_____

_____

To stop the fixer/depressor cycle and reduce the turmoil in your life, defuse the depressor and find the requirement that lies beneath the surface. With a quiet I-System, your powerful self will be in charge of your work, relationships, and play.

THE DRIVING FORCE OF ADDICTION: THE DEPRESSOR/FIXER CYCLE

When the I-System is active, it causes your behavior to be excessively driven. When you act out addictively or are driven relentlessly toward certain goals, your fixer is in the driver's seat. When you feel weak, anxious, and powerless, the depressor is in the driver's seat. The depressor and fixer have an interesting relationship. You automatically strengthen one when you push away, reject, or deny the other. For example, when you don't recognize the passive, weak, helpless thoughts the depressor has captured, the fixer becomes more energized. When you deny or fail to recognize your behavior caused by the fixer, this results in negative depressor thoughts and unpleasant body sensations. The depressor/fixer cycle is the driving force of your addiction. When the I-System is quiet, this means your depressor and fixer are no longer active, your true self is in the driver's seat, and you are no longer in an addicted mode.

Let's look more closely at the depressor/fixer cycle.

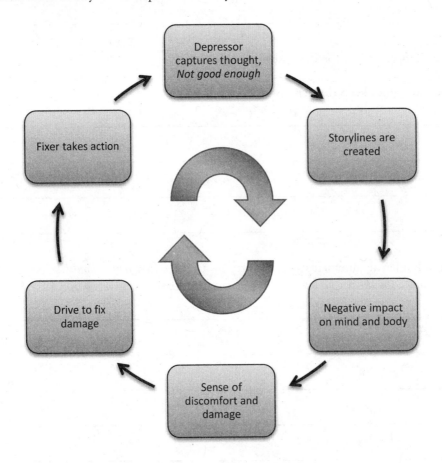

Figure 4.1 Depressor/fixer cycle

Notice that whatever the fixer does will never be good enough for the depressor.

In this exercise you will have the opportunity to explore a situation that activated your depressor/fixer cycle in detail.

1. Write down a situation that really got your I-System going (for example, *Passed over for promotion*).

_____

2. In each of the boxes below, write down the progression of your I-System activity:

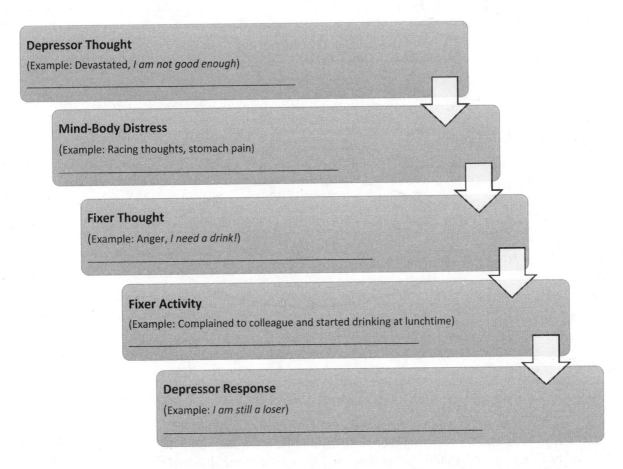

Depressor Thought
(Example: Devastated, *I am not good enough*)
_____

Mind-Body Distress
(Example: Racing thoughts, stomach pain)
_____

Fixer Thought
(Example: Anger, *I need a drink!*)
_____

Fixer Activity
(Example: Complained to colleague and started drinking at lunchtime)
_____

Depressor Response
(Example: *I am still a loser*)
_____

Notice that the depressor response in the last box only enhances the activity of the depressor and further promotes storyline and fixer activity.

3. Think back over your life. Do you recognize how pervasive your depressor/fixer's vicious cycle has been over the years? Do you see how central that cycle is in your addiction? Yes _____ No _____

List some examples of your depressor/fixer cycle:

_____

_____

WHICH TO-DOS ARE CAUSING YOU STRESS

We all have a list of to-dos that are part of our daily activities. The next two-part map shows you how your fixer is making it harder to get through your list without stress or avoidance.

1. Around the oval, jot down all the things you need to get done over the next few days that are causing you stress. Write for a couple of minutes, without editing your thoughts. The following sample map may be helpful.

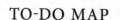

TO-DO MAP

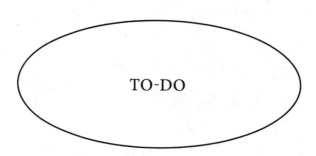

TO-DO

A. Next to each item on your map, note your level of body tension, using one of these symbols: Ø for no body tension, + for mild, ++ for moderate, or +++ for severe. It may help to see the sample map that follows. Those items with body tension are fixers.

B. List the storylines associated with the three fixers that have the most body tension:

_____

_____

_____

    These fixer-driven everyday activities are preventing you from healing your addiction. No matter how clean and sober you are, if your I-System is active in your daily activities, it prevents you from living your best life. The fixer can never fix your toxic shame.

SAMPLE MAP: TO DO

Have company over for dinner +++

Finalize plans for the new project at work +++

Pay my bills ++

See my therapist ++

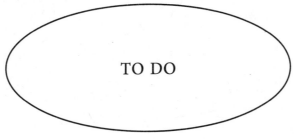

TO DO

*Go to the parent-teacher
conference +++*

*Meet with my recovery sponsor
+*

Get car serviced +

Call Mom +++

Exercise ++

Sample storylines:

Call Mom: *I should call her now. Nothing satisfies her. She criticizes me. She always tells me how to live my life.*

Go to the parent-teacher conference: *Charlie won't do his homework. His teacher always blames me. She talks down to me.*

Finalize plans for the new project at work: *My boss keeps changing the plan. I can't leave anything out. What if I make a mistake? This could end my career.*

2. Now do the map again, this time using your bridging awareness practices, and see what happens. Before you start writing, listen to background sounds, feel your body's pressure on your seat, sense your feet on the floor, and feel the pen in your hand. Take your time. Once you're settled, keep feeling the pen in your hand and start writing. Scatter your thoughts around the oval. Watch the ink go onto the paper, and listen to background sounds. Write for a couple of minutes.

TO-DO MAP WITH BRIDGING

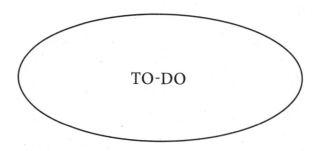

A. Compare the two maps. What do you notice?

_____

B. In this mind-body state, how do you experience your to-do list?

_____

_____

The release of body tension, and the reduced mind clutter and sense of urgency, mean that you have shifted into natural functioning. You learned that it was the depressor/fixer cycle, with its related story-lines, that made you feel overwhelmed and filled with body tension and mental pressure, not what you have to do. Without the I-System adding to your distress and taking away your self-power, you manage the things you have to do smoothly and naturally.

Now that you have calmed your I-System, it's time for you to take care of your to-do list with your true self in charge. You will gradually observe that each activity can give you a sense of well-being and peace of mind. You are fully capable of living your best life.

UNMASKING YOUR FIXER

Your days are filled with activities. Many of them may be free of cravings, fear, and anxiety (for example, playing with your dog, or watching your favorite TV show). Others (for example, rushing to an appointment or meeting, pushing yourself to meet a deadline, dealing with a never-ending list of demands for your time) could well come with body tension and storylines. When you unmask the fixer, your activities that were filled with body tension and urgency are now carried out with a quiet I-System. It may even be the same activity. It's not what you do, but who is doing it (true self or damaged self). Even positive-looking activity done with an active I-System supports your damaged self and addicted mode.

Think back over the last twenty-four hours and notice the specific body tension, mental pressure, or feelings of being driven. That's your fixer in action. See the different characteristics of body tension (location, type, or both) that come with your fixer.

Activity	Body Tension and Location	Storyline	Fixer-Driven Thought
Straighten up the garage.	Tense neck, chest pressure	It's so disorganized, I'll never get it finished.	If I really work at it, I'll get it perfect.

The fixer may also be involved when you can't seem to move on from an issue. Maybe at night, when you're trying to sleep, thoughts about whether you did or didn't do something play over and over in your mind. Your I-System's fixer is in high gear, interfering with your sleep as you try to figure the situation out or plan to fix it. Doing a two-part What's on My Mind map (see chapter 2) before bed is very helpful. Remember to also use bridging awareness practices and thought labeling to get a good night's sleep.

WHEN YOU AVOID AND PROCRASTINATE

1. Many recovering addicts tend to procrastinate and avoid getting things done that matter in their lives. Procrastination is the result of an overactive I-System. Write in the oval something that you are avoiding or putting off doing. For several minutes, jot down around the oval any thoughts that come up about that situation.

> ## WHAT I WANT TO AVOID MAP

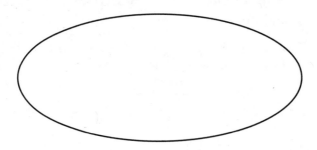

A. Describe your initial body tension and mind clutter:

_____

_____

B. List your depressors and storylines:

_____

_____

C. List your requirements:

_____

_____

D. In this mind-body state, how do you feel and act?

_____

2. You just experienced how your I-System works. It makes you anxious and prevents you from doing things. Let's do the map again, this time using your bridging awareness practices, and see what happens. Write the same goal in the oval. Before you start writing, listen to background sounds, feel your body's pressure on your seat, sense your feet on the floor, and feel the pen in your hand. Take your time. Once you're settled, keep feeling the pen in your hand, and start writing. Scatter your thoughts around the oval. Watch the ink go onto the paper, and listen to background sounds. Write for a couple of minutes.

WHAT I WANT TO AVOID MAP WITH BRIDGING

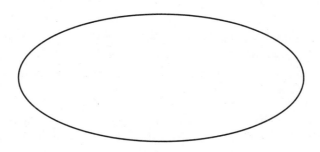

Look at the items on your map. The thoughts that come without excess body tension, anxiety, and mental pressure indicate executive functioning and the presence of your powerful self. What are they?

_____

_____

_____

Both maps you just did had the same item in the oval. In the first map, you saw how your I-System adds mind clutter, body tension, and depressor/fixer activity. In the second map, you quieted your I-System with your bridging awareness tools and shifted into natural functioning. In this state, your true self is in control. When your I-System is at rest, you have the choice of doing or not doing the things you previously wanted to avoid. Everything you do with a quiet I-System supports your recovery.

DEFUSING YOUR FIXER

Your day consists of one activity after another. Each activity you are doing or not doing throughout the day is either from natural functioning or driven by the fixer. Fixer-driven activities support your addiction; activities done while naturally functioning support your recovery. The only time you can defuse and stop your fixer is in the midst of an activity. When you stop the depressor/fixer cycle and calm your I-System, your powerful self controls the activity. Throughout the day, notice the activity of your fixer: body tension, mental pressure, the depressor/fixer cycle, and storylines. When your fixer is active, use these steps to defuse it:

1. As soon as you notice any body tension, mental urgency, and spinning negative storylines, know that your fixer is in action.

2. Use bridging awareness practices and thought labeling to quiet your I-System.

3. Be on the lookout for new stories that the I-System's fixer (or embedded depressor) may spin about how the fixer can help you. These storylines impair your judgment and cause behaviors that reinforce your addiction.

4. When the fixer is active, find the depressor that lies beneath the surface. Know that the fixer's real motive is to try to relieve the pain and dysfunction caused by the depressor (damaged self). When you defuse the depressor, you automatically reduce the pressure and urgency of the fixer and shift into your true self.

5. Remember, it's not the activity you are doing but who's doing it that is important. If it is your damaged self, your behaviors will be accompanied by body tension and mental pressure. If it's your true self, with natural functioning, your activities will be free of body tension and mental pressure.

You know when you have defused your fixer, because your I-System is quiet, your body is calm, and your activities are being done by your true self, not the pressure-driven fixer. You witness firsthand that the shame-based damaged self is a false belief. You are not broken and don't need fixing. Natural functioning is your birthright.

In the heat of any situation, you, too, can convert the fixer into natural functioning. Remember, the only time to defuse and stop your fixer is *during* an activity. Use your fixer recognition tools for several days and then fill out the chart below.

Activity	Telltale Signs of Your Fixer	Anxiety Reduction Tools You Used	Results
Running late for work.	Breathing faster, shoulders pulled up, do-or-die sense of urgency	Listened to background sounds, stayed aware of my body.	Arrived relaxed a couple of minutes late.
Avoiding going to social event.	Avoidance of something I wanted to do	Noticed underlying depressor, "I'm awkward and socially inept." Did two-part map.	Felt less anxious and went to event. Had a good time without using.

We are so used to our fixer pushing us that we have come to accept what it does with an *It's just me* attitude. How many times have you felt anxious, driven, or inhibited, and dismissed it as *It's just me*? Remember, when your I-System is on, you can defuse your fixer by simply being aware that it is active. Doing a two-part map is very helpful. Then use your bridging awareness tools to bring your awareness back to what you were doing. The tough part is noticing the early signs of your active depressor and fixer. To do this, it helps to have a strong daily bridging awareness practice. Then as soon as you start to have body tension, negative storylines, mental pressure, and feelings of being pushed, you know it's the fixer. Using all your recovery tools in everyday life helps you to gradually overcome fixer-driven daily activities and heals your addiction. Your addiction will not be cured by the event of your refusing a drink; it can only be cured by you accessing your wellspring of healing, goodness, and wisdom in your usual activities of daily living.

YOU ARE NOT BROKEN AND DON'T NEED FIXING

As you have seen on the How I Am Going to Improve My Life map, the fixer tries to present itself as a valued helper. Many people believe that their success in life is due to the drive and pressure of the fixer, and even say, "If it weren't for all this tension, I would never have accomplished anything." The truth of the matter is: an active fixer drives your addicted mode.

1. Do a map titled "What Will Happen If I Give Up My Fixer." Jot down whatever comes to mind when you imagine giving up your fixer (for example, *I'll be taken advantage of, I'll lose my job, I'll never accomplish anything*, or *I'll be a wreck*). Write for a couple of minutes. Describe your body tension at the bottom of the map.

WHAT WILL HAPPEN IF I GIVE UP MY FIXER MAP

WHAT WILL HAPPEN IF
I GIVE UP MY FIXER?

Body Tension: _____

A. Look at your map and list some of your requirements:

_____

_____

B. In this mind-body state, how do you act?

_____

Some people become anxious when they do this map. They have come to rely on the fixer to face and control situations that make them uncomfortable. They feel as if they'll lose who they are and become weak if they give up their fixers. People think, *To give up my fixer would be like giving up my right arm!* and *If I let my fixer go, I'll go right down the tubes and use.* They fear that if they relax, they will be powerless and fail. This reliance on the fixer's power is the I-System's false promise that can never be fulfilled because enough will never be enough. The next map will demonstrate that when you quiet your I-System, you free yourself from the tyranny of your fixer and experience your self-healing powers.

2. Do the previous map again, this time using your bridging awareness practices. Before you start writing, listen to background sounds, feel your body's pressure on your seat, sense your feet on the floor, and feel the pen in your hand. Take your time. Once you're settled, keep feeling the pen in your hand, and start writing. Watch the ink go onto the paper, and listen to background sounds. Write for a couple of minutes.

WHAT WILL HAPPEN IF I GIVE UP MY FIXER MAP WITH BRIDGING

WHAT WILL HAPPEN IF I GIVE UP MY FIXER?

A. List two fixer-driven behaviors that have caused difficulties in your life:

_____

_____

B. Are you ready to let go of them?   Yes _____   No _____

C. When you are in executive-functioning mode instead of in the spin of the I-System, do you feel that you are not broken and don't need fixing?   Yes _____   No _____

With a resting I-System, your powerful self is in the driver's seat. In this unified mind-body state, you have access your wellspring of healing, goodness, and wisdom, which gives you the strength and energy to take care of yourself and be clean and sober.

WHO IS DOING IT?

"What should I do?" and "How should I manage my addiction?" are questions that addicts frequently ask. But they aren't the most important questions. The real issue is not *what* you should do or *how* you should do it, but *who* is doing it: your damaged self (active I-System) or your naturally functioning true self. If your I-System is overactive and your damaged self is in charge, then you will have body tension and mental pressure. In this state, you inhabit an addicted mode. When your I-System is quiet, your true self is in the driver's seat, calmly taking the best action to deal with any situation as it arises. Here and now, with an I-System at rest, is the only time and place you can heal your addiction and live your best life.

During the day, ask yourself who is doing the activity (walking, parenting, using the computer, paying bills, doing your job, working a program, playing, and so forth). Is it your damaged self, driven by an overactive I-System, or is it your natural true self? You do not have to search for your true self. It is always present when your I-System is resting. Remember, it's not the activity but who's doing it that matters. Awareness of who's doing an activity helps you shift from the damaged self to the true self. Try it and describe what happened:

_____

_____

_____

_____

_____

_____

DON'T LET YOUR FIXER FOOL YOU

The I-System is not a static system; it may try to fool you by creating more fixers. For your continued progress, it's important to recognize new fixers as they come up. Some examples are:

I'm doing better, so I can relax and not do as much bridging.

Now that I am clean and sober, I don't need to work a recovery program.

It's okay to have one drink once in a while if the situation calls for it.

I only need to bridge when I'm experiencing my addicted mode.

Avoiding things is okay.

These fixers parade themselves as choices that come from natural functioning. But they have the same distinct signs you learned earlier in this chapter: body tension, mental pressure, urgent storylines, and not seeing the effects of your actions. What is new is that they offer themselves in a way that makes you feel good about them, and you fail to notice the higher level of tension that is driving the choice. The fixer takes the path of least resistance. When you recognize the fixer and reduce your tension with your bridging awareness practices, your true self makes the choice, free of the influence of the I-System.

REVIEW

Discover

- How your fixer drives your substance abuse and daily activities.

- How your vicious depressor/fixer cycle is perpetuating your addiction.

Experience

- When the depressor/fixer cycle is in play, these I-System partners create a vicious cycle, keeping the I-System going and sustaining your addiction.

- When you are feeling urges and cravings, or when your daily activities are filled with overactive, never-ending thoughts of how to fix yourself and the world, your fixer is in charge.

- When you become clearly aware (at the time you are doing something) that your fixer is active and use your recovery tools, you defuse your fixer (take away its power). Right away, you feel a shift from a stressful, addicted mode to one with a ready and relaxed mind and body. You can now calmly take care of yourself and whatever you have to do in natural functioning.

Apply

Remember, all your actions throughout the day are either from natural functioning or driven by the fixer. Recall that once a requirement (rule) is broken, the I-System is active. The depressor then grabs negative thoughts, spinning them into storylines that lead to an unpleasant mind-body state. Next the fixer jumps in to try to repair this negative state. When you recognize your I-System at work and then use your recovery tools, your true self is back in the driver's seat.

Colin has been in recovery for his heroin addiction for three months. He recently started working as a chef in a popular restaurant. Before his shift began he would be overcome by anxiety and negative self-talk, which would continue through his working day. He also excessively drank coffee throughout his shift to help him focus, but this further increased his racing negative thoughts and anxiety. Because of the anxiety and racing thoughts he would make mistakes with his orders, and had received two formal warnings. Colin started attending a mind-body bridging class. He learned about his depressor/fixer cycle, how it created his fears, and how this I-System activity was the cause of his anxiety and self-defeating thinking. His fixer would pressure him to do a good job. His depressor would come in with negative thoughts about how he would make mistakes and how useless he was. Then his fixer would make him drink coffee excessively, to help him cope. His storylines were all about how bad he was at anything he did, and how he would never be able to create a good career for himself. When Colin mapped out his thoughts, he found his requirements were *I should never make a mistake* and *I should always be comfortable*.

These requirements were not only causing him anxiety when they were not met, but were at the root of his heroin addiction. He began to quiet his I-System by using bridging awareness practices and thought labeling as effective tools to calm down. Soon Colin was better able to focus on his work and drink less coffee. Now when Colin is cooking and his thoughts begin to spin, he recognizes that his depressor/fixer cycle is active, labels his thoughts, feels the chef knife in his hand, hears the sizzling of the food, and calmly gets on with his working day. His daily utilization of mapping and the other recovery tools solidified his recovery from heroin addiction.

Recovery Tools

➤ Recognize the depressor/fixer cycle.

➤ Defuse the fixer.

➤ Convert fixer activity into natural functioning.

MBB RATING SCALE: WHY YOUR BEST EFFORTS SEEM TO GO WRONG

Date: _____

After using the tools in this chapter for several days, check the description that most closely reflects your practice: hardly ever, sometimes, usually, or almost always.

How often do you...	Hardly Ever	Sometimes	Usually	Almost Always
Notice the fixer's never-ending pressure and tension?				
Become aware of the body sensations associated with the fixer?				
Realize that the fixer can never fix your damaged self?				
Find the depressor embedded in the fixer?				
Notice when the depressor/fixer cycle is active?				
Recognize the storylines that come with the fixer?				
Reduce your addiction symptoms by recognizing your fixer?				
Notice the difference between fixer-driven activities and activities from natural executive functioning?				
Realize that the fixer is not necessary for your success?				
Notice a reduction of your addicted mode when you defuse your fixer in real time, using your recovery tools?				
Function better at home and at work?				

List the main body sensations you have when the fixer is in control:

_____

List urging thoughts or behaviors the fixer causes:

_____

List the themes of the storylines that come with the depressor/fixer cycle:

_____

What happened when you recognized your depressor/fixer cycle and shifted into natural functioning?

_____

MBB QUALITY OF LIFE GAUGE

Date: _____

Only do this indicator when you have made a habit in your life of using the anxiety reduction tools from the first four chapters. It lets you measure your progress and keep track of your life-changing experiences.

Over the past seven days, how did you do in these areas?

Circle the number under your answer.	Not at all	Several days	More than half the days	Nearly every day
1. I've had positive interest and pleasure in my activities.	0	1	3	5
2. I've felt optimistic, excited, and hopeful.	0	1	3	5
3. I've slept well and woken up feeling refreshed.	0	1	3	5
4. I've had lots of energy.	0	1	3	5
5. I've been able to focus on tasks and use self-discipline.	0	1	3	5
6. I've stayed healthy, eaten well, exercised, and had fun.	0	1	3	5
7. I've felt good about my relationships with my family and friends.	0	1	3	5
8. I've been satisfied with my accomplishments at home, work, or school.	0	1	3	5
9. I've been comfortable with my financial situation.	0	1	3	5
10. I've felt good about the spiritual base of my life.	0	1	3	5
11. I've been satisfied with the direction of my life.	0	1	3	5
12. I've felt fulfilled, with a sense of well-being and peace of mind.	0	1	3	5

Score Key: Column Total   ____   ____   ____   ____

0–15 .... Poor

16–30 .... Fair   Total Score _____

31–45 .... Good

46 and above .... Excellent

CHAPTER 5

LEARN HOW TO TURN OFF YOUR ADDICTION SWITCH

Discover, Experience, and Apply

Discover how requirements activate your addicted mode.

Experience how defusing your requirements prevents substance abuse.

Apply the recovery tools in your daily life to reduce the activity of your I-System and heal your addiction.

Mind-Body Language

Defusing requirements: When you use all your recovery tools, you handle a situation that used to cause you distress (turn on your I-System) with a ready and relaxed mind-body. Even when the I-System's picture of how you and the world should be is not fulfilled, the defused requirement is powerless to turn on your I-System and cause you to relapse.

YOUR OFF/ON ADDICTION SWITCH

The I-System, like a light switch, is either off or on. The natural state of the I-System is off. When it's off, you are naturally functioning with your mind and body in harmony and balance. Your ability to respond to situations is at its best. This is your true self.

This harmony and balance is only disrupted when the I-System is turned on by a *requirement*. Once active, the depressor and fixer keep the I-System going. The depressor acts by slowing down or even para-lyzing your mind and body functions (perceiving, thinking, feeling, and acting). Your mind is filled with troubling thoughts and your body is heavy and lethargic. The fixer acts by excessively speeding up your mind and body. Your mind spins with anxious, pressure-driven thoughts, and your body is tense. Because you are so anxious and overstimulated, responding in a healthy way to situations is difficult. When you recognize and defuse your requirements, you control the off/on switch. Your addicted mode is only acti-vated when your I-System is active. By switching off your I-System, you move out of your addicted mode to the natural functioning state of your true self.

Figure 5.1 shows how your mind works. All thoughts naturally flow into the lower natural-function-ing loop when your I-System is switched off. In this unified mind-body state, your true self is in charge, and you live your best life. This lower loop is your birthright. No matter who you are or what you have been through, you can experience and express your true self, right here, right now. Your true self is always present and is not tainted or impaired by your past. Your true self can never be addicted. This lower loop isn't something to aim for; it's always with you, and you experience it each and every time your I-System is switched off. With your true self in charge, you can work your way through any difficult situations that may come up. For example, when you are in the natural-functioning loop and you face a new tough situ-ation, your true self has the ability to deal with the situation in the most appropriate manner available to you. Compare this to facing a new tough situation when you are in the I-System loop. Here, your coping and problem-solving skills are limited by requirements, and the actions of the depressor/fixer cycle result in impaired functioning.

All thoughts begin as natural functioning and are free of the I-System. Requirements are thoughts made into a set of rules (a picture of how you and the world should be at any moment) by your I-System. As long as events do not violate a requirement (rule), the I-System is off and all your thoughts, feel-ings, perceptions, and actions are from natural functioning. When an event breaks a requirement, the I-System becomes active, and the depressor spins negative thoughts that create unpleasant body sensations. The fixer, in turn, creates thoughts and activities to try to undo or repair the negative mind-body state (damaged self) the depressor caused. The depressor/fixer cycle not only creates your impaired function-ing; its storylines influence the mind-body representational world, which generates further requirements.

In this chapter, you will map requirements that you have for yourself, others, and situations. Don't let your I-System fool you into thinking you can do maps in your head. When you put your thoughts on paper and notice your body sensations, a powerful mind-body free-association process takes place. The unexpected thought is often the requirement that lies beneath the surface. This is where your "aha" moments can happen. Each mapping exercise is set up in a way that increases your insights into each situa-tion. The more you are in the natural-functioning loop, the quicker and easier it is to recognize and defuse your requirements as they arise in your life. Recognizing a requirement means that after you become aware of the signs of an active I-System, you are able to identify the mental rule that has been broken about how you and the world should be. To defuse a requirement means that you now face a situation that used to cause an addicted mode with a ready, relaxed mind and body. No matter what the situation is, defusing requirements keeps your I-System turned off. Making a habit of using your recovery tools means you will live more and more of your life in the addiction-free natural-functioning loop.

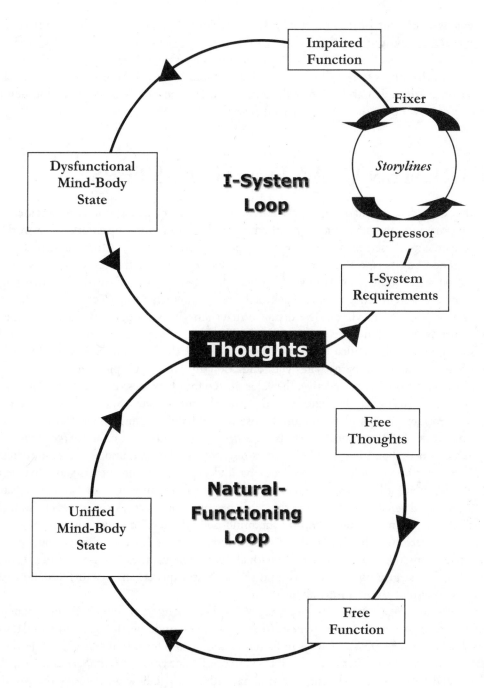

Figure 5.1 The I-System loop and the natural-functioning loop.

The mind works with thoughts. When your I-System is switched off, they flow into the natural-functioning loop, where you take care of yourself and your responsibilities. Free thoughts and free functioning are how you think, see the world, and act with an I-System at rest. When your thoughts become requirements for you and the world, you are pulled into the I-System loop, where mind-body commotion creates an unsatisfying life, lived in an addicted mode.

Since the activity of your I-System can manifest at various degrees of strength, we introduce a question that gauges the strength of your I-System. In some situations when a requirement has been triggered it generates mild I-System activity, and in other situations very strong I-System activity. When you use your recovery tools, the aim is to slow down the activity of your I-System. Sometimes you are able to stop the activity; at other times you are able to reduce it. The more you practice, the more you develop your capacity to stop or slow down the activity of your I-System.

REQUIREMENTS AND THE 12 STEPS

As you already experienced in chapter 2, at the core of your resentments are unmet requirements. In step four of 12-step programs, the main aim of a "searching and fearless moral inventory" is to work through our various resentments. Resentments are one of the primary sources of fuel that maintains your addiction. From a mind-body perspective, we can see that resentments are the result of I-System-captured expectations of ourselves, others, and the world. Once the I-System has captured these natural expectations, they become I-System requirements. Each of these requirements has accompanying depressor and fixer thoughts that become storylines. The depressor/fixer storylines rationalize and justify the requirements. Consequently, every time a requirement is not met, the I-System starts spinning and a damaged mind-body state (resentment) results. In turn, resentment keeps the I-System active. As we have seen, as long as the I-System is active, it perpetuates your addiction and keeps you prone to relapse.

From a mind-body bridging perspective, the value of step four becomes very clear. By working through our resentments and defusing requirements, we take away the fuel of our I-System. The only way to really work through resentment is to understand and defuse the underlying requirement. On the surface, some resentments may look entirely rational, such as *I resent Frank because he told a lie about me*. Of course nobody wants to be lied about, but it only becomes resentment when the underlying requirement (*Frank shouldn't tell lies about me*) is violated. When your natural expectation that others shouldn't lie becomes captured by the I-System, it becomes a requirement. Then, when it is unmet, your I-System creates mind-body distress (damaged self) and you blame the other person, which causes resentments. By recognizing and defusing your requirement, you minimize the mind-body distress and give yourself more options to deal with the other person's behavior. What drives the resentment is not the other person's act, but your mind-body distress caused by your I-System. As with all requirements, these are I-System-captured natural expectations. We do not give up our personal and relationship expectations or our likes and dislikes; we only give up our I-System requirements about them.

For those who are engaged in a 12-step program, when doing step four, it is important to be on the lookout for the requirements and depressor/fixer storylines underneath each resentment. Narcotics Anonymous' book *It Works: How and Why*, in its discussion of step four, states that "[w]e need to change how we perceive the world and alter our role in it" (Narcotics Anonymous World Services, Inc., 1993, 37). By recognizing and defusing requirements, we automatically "change how we perceive the world." When we move away from trying to conform reality to our I-System requirements and fixer-driven behaviors, we "alter our role in it." This naturally functioning mind-body state resulting from a resting I-System is in line with one of the central aims of the twelve steps, in which we let go of attempts to control what cannot be controlled. The illusion of false control is always driven by requirements.

KEEP YOUR ADDICTION SWITCH OFF IN A DISTRESSING EXPERIENCE

1. There are times when someone's behavior creates a stressful situation. Map the most distressing recent experience resulting from the behavior of another person. Write the behavior at the top of the map (*My parents insist that I take a weekly drug test*), and write how you wanted that person to act (*My parents shouldn't insist that I take a weekly drug test*) in the oval. Take a couple of minutes to write your thoughts, like *They don't trust me*, around the oval as you think about that person's behavior.

DISTRESSING EXPERIENCE MAP

Other Person's Behavior: _____

A. What is your body tension and how does it progress?

_____

B. Is your distress and behavior due to the other person's behavior or the requirement in the oval?

_____

C. How do you act in this mind-body state?

_____

D. Is your I-System on or off? _____ If it's on, rate your I-System activity from 1 to 10: _____

If you believe that your distress and behavior were a result of the other person's behavior, you are letting yourself be a victim of what has happened. As long as you do not see that how you wanted the other person to act is *your* requirement, you will suffer distress and stay in the I-System loop. When you recognize your requirement and see what it is doing to you, you start a dramatic mental and physical shift so that you are no longer a victim of other people's behavior.

91

2. Write the same behavior on the following line. In the oval again, write how you wanted that other person to act. Before you continue writing, listen to background sounds, feel your body's pressure on your seat, sense your feet on the floor, and feel the pen in your hand. Take your time. Once you feel settled, keep feeling the pen in your hand and start writing. Watch the ink go onto the paper, and listen to background sounds. Write for a couple of minutes.

DISTRESSING EXPERIENCE MAP WITH BRIDGING

Other Person's Behavior: _____

A. How is this map the same as or different from the previous map?

_____

B. How do you act in this mind-body state?

_____

C. Are you a victim of circumstance?   Yes _____   No _____

D. Is your I-System on or off? _____   If it's on, rate your I-System activity from 1 to 10: _____

On the first map in this exercise, the statement in the oval was a requirement, because it switched on your I-System. After using your bridging awareness tools to quiet your I-System, that same statement stopped being a requirement. It became a natural thought or expectation, because your I-System was calm and your body tension and mind clutter were greatly reduced. You are now ready to deal with that same situation with a clear mind and relaxed body. Your mind-body bridging practice doesn't take away your natural expectations of how others should behave, but it does remove the distress that your requirements cause.

FINDING REQUIREMENTS THAT CAUSE YOUR DISTRESS

List the situations from the past few days that caused you to experience distress and triggered your addicted mode. Realize that it's always the underlying requirement that you weren't yet aware of, and not the event, that's causing your distress. Recognizing your underlying requirement prompts changes in your thoughts and actions, and takes away your fixer-driven urges. The only way to prevent your I-System and addiction from running your life is to recognize and defuse the underlying requirements that sustain your I-System.

Situation	How You Handled the Situation	Unfulfilled Requirement
My girlfriend said I'll never change.	I started shaking and stormed out of the room.	My girlfriend should not say that I'll never change. She should accept me as I am.
The owner of the company visited our office and asked to speak to me.	I was so nervous my sweaty hands shook and I could barely speak.	I should be calm, cool, and collected when meeting the company owner. I shouldn't be put on the spot.

HANDLE A STRESS-FILLED DAY WITH YOUR I-SYSTEM SWITCH OFF

1. Think about the most stress-filled day you've had in the last several weeks. The higher your levels of stress, the more prone you are to cravings and moving into an addicted mode. Jot down whatever comes to mind when you think about that day. Write for a couple of minutes. Describe your body tension at the bottom of the map.

> ### STRESS-FILLED DAY MAP

STRESS-FILLED DAY

A. Describe your body tension and its progression:

_____

B. How do you feel and act in this mind-body state?

_____

C. Identify the requirements on your map:

_____

_____

D. Is your I-System on or off? _____ If it's on, rate your I-System activity from 1 to 10: _____

2. Do this map using your bridging awareness practices. Write about the same stress-filled day. Before you continue writing, listen to any background sounds, feel your body's pressure on your seat, sense your feet on the floor, and feel the pen in your hand. Take your time. Once you feel settled, keep feeling the pen in your hand, and start writing. Watch the ink go onto the paper, and listen to any background sounds. For the next few minutes, jot down whatever thoughts pop into your mind.

STRESS-FILLED DAY MAP WITH BRIDGING

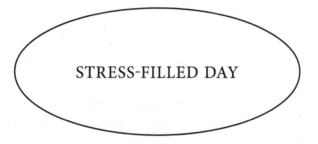

A. What is the difference between the two maps?

_____

_____

B. Can you see that it's your active I-System, not the situation, that's causing you distress?
Yes _____ No _____

C. In real time, which recovery tools will you use to stay in natural functioning while dealing with stressful situations?

_____

D. Is your I-System on or off? _____ If it's on, rate your I-System activity from 1 to 10: _____

You now know firsthand that it's your active I-System, not you or your situation, that causes your stress and suffering and keeps you from experiencing your true self. This map also shows the power of a strong daily bridging awareness practice. When you feel body tension, use your bridging awareness practices and recovery tools to create the emotional space you need to defuse requirements and deal with relationship problems and tough situations during your busy day.

MY PERFECT WORLD: POSSIBLE OR IMPOSSIBLE?

Do a How My World Would Look If My Requirements Were Met map. Scatter your thoughts around the oval for a couple of minutes. Be as specific as you can (for example, *I wouldn't be addicted, I would love myself, My family would be more understanding of my addiction, I would not worry about money*).

> ### HOW MY WORLD WOULD LOOK IF MY REQUIREMENTS WERE MET MAP

HOW MY WORLD WOULD
LOOK IF MY REQUIREMENTS
WERE MET

A. Looking back over your map, what do you notice?

_____

_____

_____

B. Is your I-System on or off? _____ If it's on, rate your I-System activity from 1 to 10: _____

Even if you and your partner, boss, friends, and neighbors met all your requirements, your active I-System would always create new mental rules about how you and the world should be at any moment. Defusing requirements is a skill that helps you keep the I-System quiet and keeps your true self in charge.

RECOGNIZE AND DEFUSE REQUIREMENTS TO PREVENT SUBSTANCE ABUSE

When distress overwhelms you and cravings flare up, that means you have a requirement that you aren't yet aware of. Use these steps to help you recognize and defuse your requirements:

1. Be aware of the first signs that your I-System is active (for example, notice specific body tension and then the depressor, fixer, and anxious storyline activity). Let these signs prompt you to look for the requirement that lies beneath the surface.

2. Practice recognizing and defusing requirements that come up in simple situations. As it becomes easier, begin to use your skills in more complex relationships and situations.

3. Use your thought labeling and bridging awareness practice tools to stop the commotion of the I-System and then find the requirement that lies beneath the surface. Remind yourself that it's *your* requirement about the activity, person, or situation—*not* the activity, person, or situation—that's causing your distress.

4. Once you feel a release of body tension and mind clutter (whether over time or suddenly) about the situation, you have quieted your I-System and shifted into natural functioning. The turmoil that used to be out of control melts into something that you can manage better. This is proof that you have recognized your requirement for that situation. Facing that same situation again without distress means you have defused that requirement.

Describe what happened when you used your recovery tools in real time to recognize your requirements in a situation that filled you with distress or activated your addicted mode.

_____

_____

Describe a situation when you prevented relapse from happening by defusing a requirement.

_____

_____

When you quiet your I-System and defuse your requirements, you are in the natural-functioning loop (figure 5.1), where your true self is in charge. In this state it is easier to handle the situation. Remember that it is not what you are doing that is causing your distress, but rather who is doing it, your damaged self or your true self.

DIFFICULT-TO-DEFUSE REQUIREMENTS

Your I-System has been very busy defining how you and your world should be. Some requirements are easy to defuse, while others haven't budged. For the requirements that are harder for you to defuse, it helps to first focus on the situation (for example, going to your wife's company party) that triggered your requirement (for example, *I shouldn't have to go to the party*) and then break that situation or thought down into smaller parts. Break the overall requirement down into many smaller, specific requirements: *I should not have cravings at a party, My wife should not leave me alone with people I don't know, I shouldn't worry so much about meeting her coworkers*. When you uncover the set of specific requirements associated with this situation, use your recovery tools on each of them. Remember, after you recognize a requirement, it's ready to be defused in real time.

Over the next few days, recognize and defuse your requirements as they come up.

Describe which recovery tools worked best for you:

_____

List the requirements you were able to defuse and those you were not able to defuse:

Was Able to Defuse	Could Not Defuse
I should not be anxious in a fellowship meeting.	*My girlfriend should be more understanding.*

In dealing with a requirement like *My girlfriend should be more understanding*, the goal of mind-body bridging is not to get your girlfriend to be more understanding, but to defuse your requirement that she should be more understanding. By doing so, you shift into natural functioning and can use your natural wisdom to relate to your girlfriend in a different way. Remember, figure 1.1 illustrates how your ability to do this expands. Use your recovery tools to recognize and defuse your requirements when the situation comes up again.

LET GO OF YOUR REQUIREMENTS

1. Do a What Will Happen If I Let Go of All My Requirements for My World map. Write your thoughts around the oval for several minutes.

WHAT WILL HAPPEN IF I LET GO OF ALL MY REQUIREMENTS FOR MY WORLD MAP

WHAT WILL HAPPEN
IF I LET GO OF ALL
MY REQUIREMENTS FOR
MY WORLD?

A. Does the commotion of your I-System leave you feeling weak and anxious, and believing that you will lose control of your life? Yes _____ No _____ If the answer is yes, you have the underlying requirement *I shouldn't let go of all my requirements.*

B. Write your level of body tension by each item on the map, using Ø for none, + for minimal, ++ for moderate, or +++ for severe. Next, put a "D" beside each item that has negative storylines and unpleasant body sensation. Observe how the depressor pushes you into the fixer. Write down your fixer above the depressor on the map and place an "F" next to it. Then list any other remaining requirements you can find below. See the sample map that follows.

Item	Requirement

Once your I-System is switched on, the activity of your depressor/fixer cycle makes it more difficult to defuse requirements.

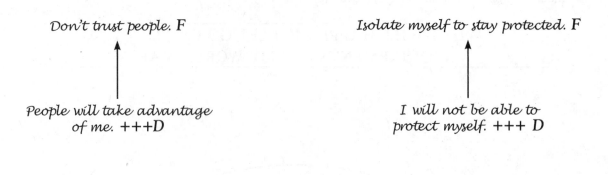

SAMPLE MAP: WHAT WILL HAPPEN IF I LET GO OF
ALL MY REQUIREMENTS FOR MY WORLD

Don't trust people. F

Isolate myself to stay protected. F

*People will take advantage
of me.* +++D

*I will not be able to
protect myself.* +++ D

WHAT WILL HAPPEN
IF I LET GO OF ALL
MY REQUIREMENTS FOR
MY WORLD?

*Things will go more
smoothly.* Ø

Take more classes. F

Temptation to use. F

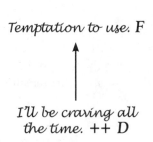

*I'll never be able to
do anything.* +++ D

*I'll be craving all
the time.* ++ D

Item	Requirement
I will not be able to protect myself.	*I should protect myself.*
People will take advantage of me.	*People shouldn't take advantage of me.*

2. Do the map again, this time using your bridging awareness practices. Before you start writing, listen to background sounds, feel your body's pressure on your seat, sense your feet on the floor, and feel the pen in your hand. Take your time. Once you're settled, keep feeling the pen in your hand, and start writing your thoughts. Watch the ink go onto the paper, and listen to background sounds. Write for a couple of minutes.

> WHAT WILL HAPPEN IF I LET GO OF ALL MY REQUIREMENTS FOR MY WORLD MAP WITH BRIDGING

WHAT WILL HAPPEN
IF I LET GO OF ALL MY
REQUIREMENTS FOR
MY WORLD?

What are the differences between the two maps?

_____

_____

_____

_____

Is it getting clearer that having I-System requirements is harmful to you and your world? Requirements limit your ability to deal with other people and situations. When you quiet your I-System, your powerful natural self can respond in an active, attentive, and healthy way in your relationships and situations. You'll be able to face each moment with full access to your inner wellspring of healing, goodness, and wisdom. Your true self will be in charge of your recovery.

Use all your recovery tools to reduce the activity of your I-System in real time and prevent relapses.

101

REVIEW

Discover

- How requirements activate your addicted mode.

- How requirements lead to resentments.

- How it feels when a requirement is defused.

- How defusing your requirements prevents substance abuse.

Experience

- When you use all your recovery tools, you handle a situation that previously caused you distress (activated I-System) with a ready and relaxed mind-body. Even when the I-System's picture of how you and the world should be is not fulfilled, the requirement is powerless to turn on your I-System and cause you to relapse.

- How the I-System activity scale helps you gauge the various degrees of strength of your I-System activity. In some situations when a requirement has been triggered, it generates mild I-System activity, and in other situations, very strong I-System activity. The more you practice, the more you develop your capacity to slow down or stop the activity of your I-System.

Apply

Tony, a twenty-five-year-old office worker and recovering methamphetamine addict, gradually became unable to function in his job because of his depressive episodes. His low energy levels, lack of motivation, and constant self-defeating thoughts made work a hell for him. After using up most of his sick leave, he took the advice of his primary care physician and sought help. He started mind-body bridging. His bridging awareness practices relieved his addiction symptoms enough that he could resume working. By mapping his distressing experiences and using other follow-up maps, Tony saw requirements, such as *No one should get angry at me* and *People should be understanding*. When these situations would happen, his storylines—*They are angry with me, I could get fired, I am a loser*—fueled his I-System and led to his symptoms. Using his recovery tools to defuse his requirements, Tony became proficient at reducing the activity of his I-System and began enjoying work.

Defusing requirements is a key recovery tool. Remember, using all of your recovery tools allows you to become good at switching off your I-System. Turning off your addiction switch gives you access to the natural functioning of your true self.

Recovery Tools

➤ Defuse your requirements for yourself, others, and situations.

MBB RATING SCALE: LEARN HOW TO TURN OFF YOUR ADDICTION SWITCH

Date: _____

After using the tool in this chapter for several days, check the description that most closely reflects your practice: hardly ever, sometimes, usually, or almost always.

How often do you...	Hardly Ever	Sometimes	Usually	Almost Always
Recognize that requirements always activate your I-System and limit your true self?				
Recognize the requirements that are responsible for your distress?				
Prevent addiction symptoms by defusing a requirement?				
See that requirements you have for others or situations trap you, keeping you from being your true self?				
Cut off storylines by using thought labeling and bridging awareness practices?				
Notice the true self when it's in charge?				
Experience the damaged self as a myth of the I-System?				
Experience your true self functioning, with your I-System is switched off?				
Know it's your true self when you are naturally functioning moment by moment?				
Come to appreciate aspects of your everyday life?				
Experience that you are connected to a wellspring of healing, goodness, and wisdom?				
Find that your relationships have improved?				
Function better at home and at work?				

List three requirements you defused that previously caused overwhelming cravings and urges or overwhelming distress. How did you deal with the situation(s) with a quiet I-System?

_____

_____

_____

CHAPTER 6

BUILD HEALTHY RELATIONSHIPS

Discover, Experience, and Apply

Discover how the I-System prevents you from having healthy relationships.

Experience how defusing your requirements for yourself improves your relationships.

Apply the recovery tools in your daily life to reduce the activity of your I-System and heal your addiction.

RELATIONSHIPS, ADDICTION, AND YOUR I-SYSTEM

The requirements of your I-System get you into relationships you shouldn't be in, keep you out of those that are good for you, and, most importantly, create stress in your present relationships. Moreover, the stress caused in relationships is a major risk factor for relapse. The application of the recovery tools in this workbook will greatly increase your capacity for healthy relationships, and if you are engaged in a 12-step program, will enhance your relationships in the fellowship.

The requirements you have for yourself constantly create inner distress, impair your self-esteem, and interfere with your relationships. You know how painful it is when others don't accept who you are. But what about the pain you put yourself through when you don't accept yourself? Can you imagine the relief you feel when your inner critic is quiet, letting your powerful self be in the driver's seat? When you defuse your persistent self-demands (requirements for yourself), you automatically silence the inner fixer critic and strengthen the foundations of your relationships. The real stressor in your relationships is neither you nor the other person, but your active I-System. Once it has been made active by a requirement (*I should be...*), your depressor pulls the rug out from under your self-esteem, making you feel small, weak, vulnerable, and inadequate. Your fixer responds by driving your addicted mode with overactive, never-ending worry and thoughts of how to fix yourself and the world. This interferes with your self-esteem, and keeps you from developing healthy relationships. When your I-System is quiet, you clearly see that your troubling thoughts are just thoughts, your body is calm, and you know the truth—you are whole and complete, not weak and damaged. This is the addiction-free base for your relationships.

It's vital to remember that defusing requirements like *He shouldn't be so demanding, My wife shouldn't speak to other men,* and *No one should show interest in my partner* doesn't mean you give up your natural expectation that you and your partner behave in an acceptable way. What it does mean is that when your partner acts in a way that used to create your addiction symptoms (because of your requirement), your natural true self will now respond to the situation in an appropriate way. If that requirement is not defused, your ability to respond remains controlled by your active I-System.

KEEP THE PAST IN THE PAST

Although your addiction has roots in the past, mind-body bridging does not try to uncover or understand the past. Instead it gives you the tools to heal your present substance abuse problems by keeping the past in the past.

1. Do a How I Got to Be the Way I Am map. Around the oval, write how you got to be the way you are. Write for a couple of minutes. A sample map follows.

HOW I GOT TO BE THE WAY I AM MAP

HOW I GOT TO BE THE
WAY I AM

A. What is your body tension?

_____

B. What storyline themes run through your map?

_____

_____

C. Describe when and how often you use these storylines—for example, when you feel anxious or calm, when you're sad or happy, or when you're bored or busy:

_____

D. Is your I-System on or off? _____   If it's on, rate your I-System activity from 1 to 10: _____

The I-System uses stories—positive and negative, about the past and future—to keep you from living in the present. No matter what they are about, storylines tense your body, limit your awareness, and pull you away from being able to take care of yourself and your responsibilities. Storylines stop your mind-body from experiencing the present moment and prevent you from healing your anxiety. Being aware of your storylines quiets your I-System and puts you in the executive-functioning loop, where thoughts of the past are simply thoughts, without the heat and spin of the I-System.

SAMPLE MAP: HOW I GOT TO BE THE WAY I AM

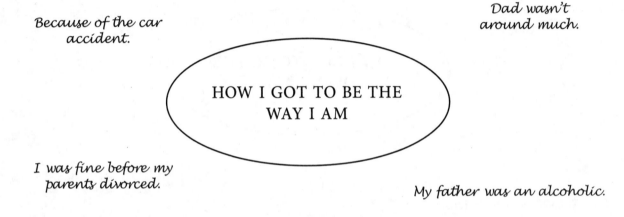

A lot of pain.

Life seemed pointless.

Poor school district.

Mom was depressed.

Dad wasn't around much.

Because of the car accident.

HOW I GOT TO BE THE WAY I AM

I was fine before my parents divorced.

My father was an alcoholic.

I was physically abused.

I never gave up.

My friends always had my back.

A. What is your body tension? *Heart beating fast, pressure in my chest.*

B. What storyline themes run through your map? *I was a victim.*

C. Describe when and how often you use these storylines: *Whenever things don't go right.*

D. Is your I-System on or off?   *On*   If it's on, rate your I-System activity from 1 to 10: *8*

2. Do another How I Got to Be the Way I Am map, this time using your bridging awareness practices. Before writing, listen to any background sounds, feel your body's pressure on your seat, sense your feet on the floor, and feel the pen in your hand. After you feel settled, jot around the oval whatever thoughts pop into your mind. Keep listening to background sounds and feeling the pen in your hand. Watch the ink go onto the paper. Write for a couple of minutes.

HOW I GOT TO BE THE WAY I AM MAP WITH BRIDGING

Husband died

Children taken from me

loss my home twice

Job losses lost loss of freedom car/lisence

HOW I GOT TO BE THE WAY I AM

married too young

Too much loss

A. How is this map different from your first How I Got to Be the Way I Am map?

I wrote more about the most current things that have happened

B. What insights have you gained from doing this bridging map?

The cycle of addiction where it starts and how it manifests and continues to grow and develope

C. Is your I-System on or off? off   If it's on, rate your I-System activity from 1 to 10: _____

WHAT STOPS YOU FROM HEALING YOUR ADDICTION

"Being in the moment" has become a popular theme for improving yourself and your relationships. But the problem is not being in the moment, because there has never been a human being who wasn't in the moment. You can only breathe now; you can only act now; your heart can't pump yesterday's blood or tomorrow's blood. It can only beat right here, right now. It's impossible not to live in the present moment. The issue is not being in the present moment or not, but rather who is in the present moment—your damaged self or your true self. The problem is that the I-System, when activated by requirements, keeps you in a state of your damaged self and pulls you away from experiencing the healing power of your natural self, right here, right now. Let's see how it works.

Do a How I Want to Be Right Here, Right Now map. Inside the circle, write how you would like to be right here, right now (for example, organized, strong, calm, confident, intelligent). Be specific! After you have listed at least six qualities, write the opposite of each quality outside the circle. Connect the quality inside the circle with a line to its opposite, outside the circle. If needed, see the sample map that follows.

HOW I WANT TO BE RIGHT HERE, RIGHT NOW MAP

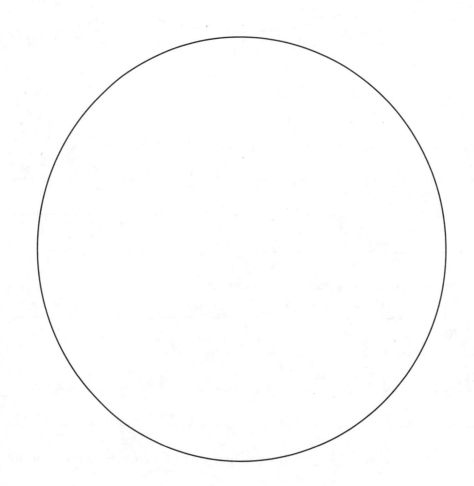

SAMPLE MAP: HOW I WANT TO BE RIGHT HERE, RIGHT NOW

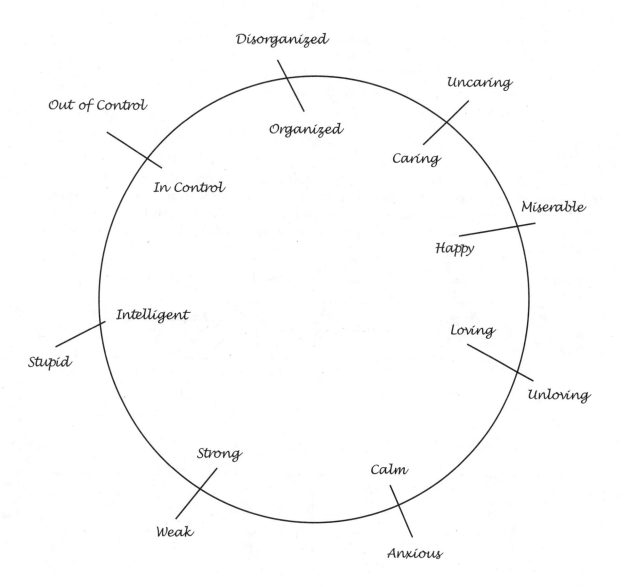

1. How do the qualities *inside* the circle make you feel?

_____

_____

_____

2. How do the qualities *outside* the circle make you feel?

_____

_____

_____

If the qualities *outside* the circle create body tension and negative emotions, they are triggers. Remember, a trigger (an event or thought) is a sign that a requirement has made your I-System active. This means that those opposite qualities (about how you want to be) *inside* the circle are requirements the I-System has created for you. Once your requirement for yourself is defused, the trigger no longer turns on your I-System.

3. From your map, list your triggers and requirements about how you "should" be:

Trigger	Requirement
Being disorganized	*I should be organized.*

When your I-System takes hold of your natural expectation, that expectation turns into a requirement (an ideal picture of who you should be). This creates mind clutter and body tension, and keeps your anxiety going. Your self-esteem suffers, and your relationships are filled with anxiety. Recognizing and defusing the requirements you have for yourself and about how you interact with others is the key to healing your addiction and improving your relationships.

MIRROR, MIRROR ON THE WALL

Did you know that poor self-image keeps your addicted mode going and affects your relationships?

1. Let's do a Mirror map. Find a quiet place and look in a mirror. Before you start writing, really look at yourself for a minute or so. Next, write around the oval any thoughts and feelings that come to mind about what you see. Try not to censor anything. Glance back at the mirror several times and keep writing whatever comes to mind. Describe your body tension at the bottom of the map.

MIRROR MAP

Body Tension: _____

A. Is your I-System on or off? _____ If it's on, rate your I-System activity from 1 to 10: _____

B. What are your storylines?

_____

_____

C. Is your depressor causing you to experience your face as an enemy and making you feel unacceptable? Yes _____ No _____

D. What are your requirements?

_____

_____

E. Describe how your self-image is related to your drinking and/or using.

_____

2. Do another Mirror map, this time using your bridging awareness practices. Before writing, listen to any background sounds, feel your body's pressure on your seat, sense your feet on the floor, and feel the pen in your hand. Now look in the mirror and keep listening to background sounds. Take your time. After you feel settled, jot around the oval whatever thoughts pop into your mind. Keep listening to background sounds and feeling the pen in your hand. Watch the ink go onto the paper. Write for a couple of minutes.

MIRROR MAP WITH BRIDGING

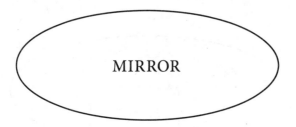

A. How is this map different from your first Mirror map?

_____

_____

B. Is your I-System on or off? _____ If it's on, rate your I-System activity from 1 to 10: _____

C. Did the facial features you see in the mirror change? Yes _____ No _____

D. Do you now have a new level of self-acceptance? Yes _____ No _____

E. How do you act when you accept yourself?

_____

Take a good look at your image in the mirror every morning and again at night. Let your thoughts flow freely, and notice your body tension. See the telltale signs of your active I-System and gauge its activity. Be aware of your depressor, your fixer, and, most importantly, your requirements for yourself. When you use your bridging awareness practices, the foundation of who you are becomes stable and your emotions balance themselves. Over time, observe how your I-System activity decreases, and your self-image improves, without your having to try to fix yourself. This shift in self-acceptance that comes with the continued use of your recovery tools makes a firm base for your recovery and for healthy relationships.

RECOVERY TOOLS TO IMPROVE YOUR SELF-IMAGE

- *Thought labeling*: When a negative thought pops into your mind, remember, a thought is just a thought. Label your negative thoughts as just thoughts, and return to what you were doing. For example, when *I'll never be good enough* pops into your mind, say to yourself, *I'm having the thought, "I'll never be good enough," and it's just a thought.*

- *Bridging awareness practices*: When you notice negative self-talk and body tension in your life, know that it is a sign that your I-System is switched on, tune in to your senses, and then go back to what you were doing.

- *Storyline awareness*: When you catch yourself going over stories about negative things that have happened to you, notice the repeating themes, recognize them as storylines, and return to the task at hand. Recognize it's the storylines and not your past that are keeping your anxiety going. You are not a victim of your past. Remember, it's not your negative thoughts that get you down or your positive thoughts that pull you up; your storylines (true or false, positive or negative) create mind clutter and fill every cell of your body with tension, keeping the depressor/fixer dance going. When your I-System gets hold of your stories, it takes you away from fully functioning in the present moment, and sets the stage for your addicted mode.

- *Mapping*: Use the two-part mind-body maps. The first map helps you find your requirements that reinforce your negative self-beliefs. Noticing your body tension is what helps you find these requirements. Use your bridging awareness practices on the second map to see the truth about negative self-beliefs and return to natural functioning.

- *Mirror mapping*: Doing a daily Mirror map (the last two-part map you just did) builds your self-esteem. After you have noticed a calming of your I-System and an improvement in your self-esteem, do a full-body Mirror map.

- *Defusing requirements*: When you notice body tension and negative self-talk, quiet your I-System, and then find your requirement. For example, if the negative self-talk is *I'm helpless*, the requirement is *I should not be helpless*. When a situation comes up and a thought enters your mind about being helpless and you have signs of body tension, your I-System has been activated by that requirement, impairing your ability to deal with the situation. To defuse the requirement, recognize that your distress is caused by the requirement and not by the situation or your negative thoughts. Once you feel a release of body tension and mind clutter (whether over time or suddenly), you know you have defused your requirement. Your powerful self is back in the driver's seat.

POWERING YOUR SELF-IMAGE IMPROVES RELATIONSHIPS

Use your recovery tools today to keep your negative self-image (negative self-belief) from filling your life with unnecessary problems. Then fill out the chart below.

Negative Self-Image	Body Tension	What Recovery Tools You Used and How	Body Sensations	How Your Behavior Changed After Using Your Tools
I'm not smart enough to get ahead in the world.	Chest tight, shallow breath	Labeled my thoughts.	Chest and breathing relaxed	Wasn't as depressed. Accomplished a lot on the job today.
I'm unlovable.	Gut cramps	I immediately recognized the thought "I should be lovable" as a requirement.	Calmer	"Light came on," day went smoothly, and I wasn't defensive or angry.

Your I-System requirements about how you "should be" are getting in the way of your self-image and of self-healing your addiction. These requirements keep you from believing and trusting in who you are, right here and now. Recall that you will never be smart enough, attractive enough, or calm enough to satisfy a requirement. When the requirement isn't satisfied, your I-System heats up with negative thoughts and body tensions. This affects not only how you feel about yourself, but also how you act in your relationships. No matter who you are or what you have been through, your mind-body recovery tools can strengthen your self-image, heal your addiction, and improve your relationships.

REQUIREMENTS FOR YOURSELF KEEP YOU FROM HEALING YOUR ADDICTION

1. List three situations from the last several days where your requirements for yourself—for example, *I should know the answer when my boss asks me a question, I should be home on time, I shouldn't be alone, I shouldn't make a mistake*—activated your I-System.

Situation	Requirement for Yourself
At our morning meeting, my boss asked me a question.	I should know the answer when my boss asks me a question.

2. Fill out this chart based on what you listed in the chart above:

Body Tension and Its Progression When Your Requirement Is Met	Body Tension and Its Progression When Your Requirement Is *Not* Met
Stomach tight, foot jiggles, hands grip chair arms tightly	Face hot, dry mouth, pressure builds in chest

117

3. Fill out the next chart for each requirement from the previous one:

Storylines When Meeting Requirement	Storylines When Not Meeting Requirement
It's a relief, It's over, What will happen next time, It's always the same.	I'll never have all the answers, I'm stupid, I may lose my job.

4. Fill out the next chart using the same requirements:

Your Behavior When Meeting Requirement	Your Behavior When Not Meeting Requirement
Felt relieved, but worried about next time.	Anxious and depressed all day. Made mistakes.

The I-System has you between a rock and a hard place. When your requirements for yourself aren't met, your depressor moves into the driver's seat, leaving you powerless and filled with urges and cravings. Even when you are able to meet your requirements, the fixer moves into the driver's seat, and enough is never enough. It's not a matter of meeting or not meeting your requirements, but one of defusing them. When your requirements are defused, your true self is in the driver's seat, and you naturally take the right action moment by moment.

5. Using your bridging awareness practices, listen to background sounds, feel your body's pressure on your seat, sense your feet on the floor, and feel the pen in your hand. When you're settled, label your thoughts and go over each requirement you listed in the first chart in this exercise. What has happened to each of the requirements after mind-body bridging?

Requirement One:

_____

Requirement Two:

_____

Requirement Three:

_____

YOUR EVERYDAY RELATIONSHIPS

Now that you know how critical it is for your self-esteem and well-being that you have a quiet I-System, it's time to tackle your relationships. We all have natural hopes and desires for ourselves and others (to be respectful, dependable, supportive, honest, helpful, and so forth). Each of us uses these natural expectations to guide us as we interact with others. When the I-System takes hold of these expectations and makes them requirements, they harm our relationships, close off our natural executive functioning, and limit our ability to relate to others.

Let's look at what happens when your natural expectations for yourself are turned into requirements, and examine how they harm your relationships and lower your self-esteem. This exercise is about the requirements you have for yourself in your relationships with coworkers, in-laws, neighbors, grocery clerks, and so on (for example, *I shouldn't be anxious when I host the neighborhood potluck, I should get along with all of my coworkers, I should like my mother-in-law*).

Answer the following questions:

1. My relationship with _____

A. What natural expectations do you have for yourself in this relationship? Example: *I should set better boundaries with my friend.*

_____

_____

B. How do you feel and act, and what is your body tension when you don't follow through? Example: *I get anxious and worry about the relationship.*

_____

C. What are your requirements about this relationship?

_____

_____

D. Use your recovery tools to defuse your requirements and change this relationship.

2. List your natural expectations for yourself in other everyday relationships; be as specific as possible. Note if they have been made into requirements.

Natural Expectation	Body Tension If Expectation Is Not Met	Is It Now a Requirement?
I want to be a good friend.	*Knot in stomach, shoulders tight*	*Yes*
Be polite to the grocery clerk.	*None*	*No*

When your requirement isn't met, you are in distress, with your I-System creating mind clutter and body tension. Recognize your requirements and use your recovery tools to defuse them. When your natural expectation isn't met, you feel let down, but you are able to handle the situation without undue worry.

YOUR MOST IMPORTANT RELATIONSHIP

1. Map your expectations for yourself in your most important relationship. Write the person's name in the oval. Around the oval and *inside* the circle, write your thoughts about how you should be in that relationship (for example, *I should be strong, I should always be supportive, I should be grateful*). There's no right or wrong. Be specific and work quickly for the next few minutes. After you have written down how you should be, write the opposite of each quality outside the circle (for example, *Weak, Unsupportive, Ungrateful*). Connect the quality inside the circle with a line to its opposite, outside the circle.

HOW I SHOULD BE IN MY MOST IMPORTANT RELATIONSHIP MAP

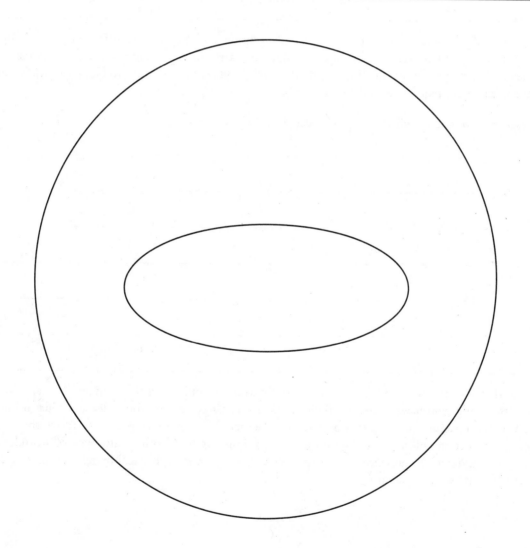

A. How do the qualities inside the circle make you feel?

_____

_____

_____

B. How do the qualities outside the circle make you feel?

_____

_____

_____

If the qualities outside the circle create body tension and negative emotions, they are triggers. Remember, a trigger (an event or thought) is a sign that a requirement has made your I-System active. This means that those opposite qualities inside the circle, about how you want to be in your most important relationship, are requirements the I-System has created for you.

C. Describe how you act when you don't meet those requirements:

_____

_____

_____

_____

_____

Now that you are aware of the requirements for yourself and know the damage they are doing to you and the world, you have the responsibility to do something about it. Your "doing" is just using your recovery tools to defuse requirements and reduce the activity of your I-System. Without this diligent doing, your addiction will not heal. You do not have to force yourself to have any type of attitude; when your I-System is quiet, the presence of your true self is more than enough. Healthy relationships heal your addiction because your I-System is at rest.

2. Do the map again, writing the person's name in the oval. Before you continue writing, listen to background sounds, feel your body's pressure on your seat, sense your feet on the floor, and feel the pen in your hand. Take your time. Once you're settled, keep feeling the pen in your hand, and start writing any thoughts that come to mind about that relationship. As you write, keep paying attention to background sounds, feeling the pen in your hand, and watching the ink go onto the paper. Write for a couple of minutes.

HOW I SHOULD BE IN MY MOST IMPORTANT RELATIONSHIP MAP WITH BRIDGING

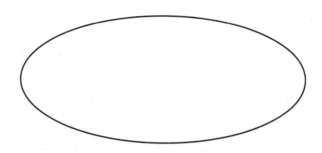

A. In this mind-body state, how do you act?

_____

_____

B. How can this map help you in your relationship?

_____

_____

The release of body tension means you have moved from the I-System loop into the natural-functioning loop (see figure 5.1), where your true self acts in a natural way. You still have thoughts or natural expectations about your relationship, but this release of body tension frees you to act in a different way.

When your active I-System switches off, you let go of your requirements and create new ways to relate in your most important relationships, free from unnecessary problems.

TRANSFORM YOUR MOST IMPORTANT RELATIONSHIP

You have been building a foundation for your relationship by defusing your requirements for yourself. Now it's time to focus on the requirements you have for the person who is most important to you.

1. Do a map of how you think the person most important to you should act. Write that person's name in the oval. Around the oval, write your thoughts for how you want that person to act. Write for a couple of minutes.

HOW THE PERSON MOST IMPORTANT TO ME SHOULD ACT MAP

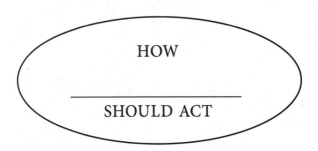

Look back over the items on the map and label your requirements with an "R." Next, under each requirement, write what storylines ("SL") you have when the other person does not meet that requirement. Below each thought, note whatever body tension ("BT") you have when the other person doesn't meet your requirement. Take your time doing this map. See the sample map that follows.

SAMPLE MAP: HOW THE PERSON MOST IMPORTANT TO ME SHOULD ACT

(R) *She should be more supportive of my recovery.*

(SL) *Recovery is difficult for me. If I get too stressed, I might relapse. I don't need to deal with her issues.*

(BT) *Tight chest*

(R) *She should like my friends.*

(SL) *She's ashamed of me.*

(BT) *Chest hurts*

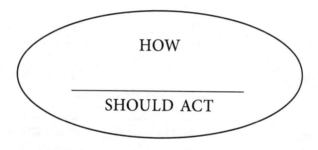

(R) *She should respect how hard I work.*

(SL) *I don't get any slack; I hate conflict and always lose.*

(BT) *Shoulders tight*

(R) *She should be more intimate.*

(SL) *She is tired of me and does not love me.*

(BT) *Stomachache*

R = Requirement

SL = Storyline when requirement is unfulfilled

BT = Body tension when requirement is unfulfilled

A. For each item on your map, fill out the following chart:

Requirement	How Do You Feel and Act When Your Important Other Doesn't Meet Your Requirement?	How Does It Affect Your Relationship?
He should respect how hard I work.	Withdraw, I worry that I am not good enough for him, I go to the bar with a friend.	Creates distance and guilty feelings.

B. Now, using your bridging awareness practices and thought labeling, when you feel settled, go back over your relationship requirements from the chart above and fill out the chart below.

Requirement	How Do You Feel and Act When Your Important Other Doesn't Meet Your Requirement?	How Does It Affect Your Relationship?
He should respect how hard I work.	Disappointed, but can talk to him.	Makes us closer.

When there is a release of body tension, it shows that you are ready to defuse your requirement when the situation comes up again. Your challenge is to use all your recovery tools daily so that when the situation comes up again, you will be able to greatly reduce the activity of your I-System.

2. Write the name of the person from the previous map in the oval below. Next, choose the requirement that still causes you the most distress when it's not met (for example, *She should respect how hard I work*) and write that on the line below. Now write your thoughts around the oval for a couple of minutes, describing how things would look if that person did meet that requirement. Use as much detail as possible. For example, if the requirement is *She should respect how hard I work*, you might write, *She would not be critical*, *She would not raise her voice*, or *She would tell me how much she loves me*.

> ## HOW THINGS WOULD LOOK IF MY REQUIREMENT WERE MET MAP

Requirement that causes me the most distress: _____

```
            HOW THINGS WOULD
                LOOK IF
         _____
           MET MY REQUIREMENT
```

A. Do you really think this will happen?   Yes _____   No _____

B. Do you recognize that an active I-System will keep creating requirements for you and your relationship?   Yes _____   No _____

Many people smile when doing this map, because they see clearly how the I-System works. They see that when they defuse their requirements, they can handle personal boundaries and basic rights from a position of strength.

WHO IS STILL CREATING STRESS FOR YOU?

Mind-body bridging is not about learning how you should relate to others; it *is* about finding out how the I-System restricts you and your relationships. Then your true self is in the driver's seat.

1. Do a requirement map for someone who is still creating the most stress for you. In the oval, write the name of the person who continues to trouble you the most. Around the oval, write your expectations for how that person should act. Write for a couple of minutes.

PERSON CREATING STRESS MAP

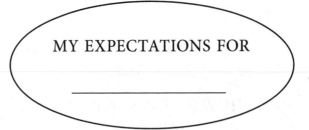

A. Next, under each item on the map, list any body tension you have when the other person does *not* meet that expectation. Those items are requirements.

B. Describe how the fixer and depressor are dancing in this relationship.

_____

C. What are your storylines?

_____

D. In this mind-body state, how do you feel and act?

_____

E. Is your I-System on or off? _____ If it's on, rate your I-System activity from 1 to 10: _____

2. Do the map again, this time using your bridging awareness practices. Write the same person's name in the oval. Before you continue writing, listen to background sounds, feel your body's pressure on your seat, sense your feet on the floor, and feel the pen in your hand. Take your time. Once you're settled, keep feeling the pen in your hand and start writing any thoughts that come to mind about how that person should act. Watch the ink go onto the paper, and keep listening to background sounds. Write for a couple of minutes.

PERSON CREATING STRESS MAP WITH BRIDGING

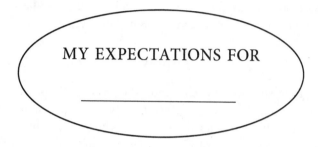

MY EXPECTATIONS FOR

_____

A. How is this map different from the previous map?

_____

B. What body sensations do you have when you imagine that person not doing what you wrote down on this map? The absence of body tension means that the item is not a requirement and that it is a natural expectation.

_____

C. In this mind-body state, how do you feel and act?

_____

D. Is your I-System on or off? _____ If it's on, rate your I-System activity from 1 to 10: _____

E. When your I-System is switched off, your natural goals and expectations do not become pressure-driven requirements. Go back to the previous map and use your recovery tools on any remaining requirements you had for that person. Do this map as often as needed. When you recognize and defuse requirements you have for both yourself and others, your powerful self, with its whole range of experiences, emotions, and gifts, enters into each and every relationship. There is no instruction manual for keeping relationships free of problems, only the golden key: an I-System at rest.

REVIEW

Discover

- That the I-System prevents you from having healthy relationships.

- That your distress is not caused by the other person's behavior or by anything lacking in you.

- That defusing your requirements for yourself and others improves your relationships.

Experience

- When you defuse requirements for yourself and others, you handle situations that used to cause distress with a ready and relaxed mind-body. Your true self is back in the driver's seat.

Apply

- Defusing your requirements for yourself creates the power to improve your relationships and heal from your addiction. When you defuse both sets of your requirements (for how you and the other person should be), your powerful self will naturally build healthy relationships. Every time you reduce the activity of your I-System, your addiction heals.

- Tools to Defuse Requirements for Yourself

  1. Be aware of the first signs that your I-System has been switched on (body tension, self-critical or anxious thoughts, or storylines). This will prompt you to look for the hidden requirement.

  2. Use your thought labeling and bridging awareness practice tools to stop the uproar of the I-System.

  3. Recognize that it's your requirement for yourself, not the other person or the situation, that's causing your distress.

  4. Use your recovery tools to find and defuse your requirement. You'll know you have defused the requirement when you feel a release of body tension and self-critical mind clutter. When the situation comes up again, your true self will be in the driver's seat, and you'll be able to deal with it in a calm and appropriate way.

Recovery tools

➢ Defuse your requirements for yourself.

➢ Defuse your requirements for your relationships.

➢ Mirror mapping

MBB RATING SCALE: BUILD HEALTHY RELATIONSHIPS

Date: _____

After using the tools in this chapter for several days, check the description that most closely reflects your practice: hardly ever, sometimes, usually, or almost always.

How often do you...	Hardly Ever	Sometimes	Usually	Almost Always
Notice that requirements always switch on your I-System, causing stress in your relationships?				
Notice that requirements keep your negative self-image going?				
Improve relationships by defusing requirements?				
See that your requirements for yourself trap you and keep your addiction going?				
Experience yourself as far more than who you thought you were?				
Notice that all you need to do to act from natural functioning is quiet your I-System?				
Notice when your damaged self is in the driver's seat?				
Experience your damaged self as a myth of the I-System?				
Recognize when you are in natural-functioning mode?				
Appreciate your powerful self (who you are when you function naturally moment by moment)?				
See everyday life in a new light by having a quiet I-System?				
Notice yourself connected to your wellspring of healing, goodness, and wisdom?				
Notice that your relationships have improved?				
Function better at home and at work?				
Notice your self-esteem increasing?				

List three requirements for yourself in your relationship that previously activated your I-System and that you now deal with by having a resting I-System:

_____

_____

_____

CHAPTER 7

TAKE CHARGE OF YOUR EMOTIONS

Discover, Experience, and Apply

Discover how your I-System causes your emotions to get out of control.

Experience how calming the I-System allows you to be in charge of your emotions.

Apply the recovery tools in your daily life to reduce the activity of your I-System and heal your addiction.

EMOTIONS AND THE I-SYSTEM

Addicts are often out of touch with their emotions, and/or overwhelmed by them. They tend to experience feelings as vague, overpowering sensations over which they perceive they have little control. Moreover, addicts are often "ill-equipped to regulate and modulate feeling" (Khantzian, in Flores 1997, 208). This lack of inner control is often a frightening experience. From this perspective, addiction is seen as a dysfunctional attempt to control an out-of-control inner world. Your substance of choice becomes our main method of mood management and temporarily restores our inner equilibrium. Because of the difficulty addicts have in regulating emotions, the experience of strong negative emotions is one of the primary causes of relapse.

Mind-body bridging provides unique methods to regulate emotions and regain control of your life. All your emotions, including negative emotions, are originally from natural functioning. When the I-System is at rest, your emotions are mind-body facts that naturally allow you to live your best life. Your natural emotions, along with your actions, express your true self. When your I-System is active, the depressor and fixer corrupt your natural emotions, and only then do they become problematic. These altered emotions create suffering, misery, and distress. The depressor takes natural emotions like sadness, disappointment, guilt, and remorse and produces negative storylines and a painful, weighed-down body. These altered emotions are no longer helpful; they become a heavy burden restricting your life. On the other hand, the fixer takes natural emotions like fear, anxiety, and anger and stirs up your body and mind. These altered emotions captured by the I-System cause you to become overly fearful, anxious, or angry, and create a state where you are bound to overreact. The bottom line is that the I-System causes these altered emotions to rule you. Your natural emotions, which are there to add depth and vitality to your life, are corrupted by the I-System and become the boss of your daily life. By using your recovery tools to quiet your I-System, your emotions automatically revert back to their natural, healthy state.

In mind-body bridging, the crucial factor in healing from your addiction is not recognizing the difference between worry, fear, and anxiety, but recognizing whether or not your I-System is switched on or off. When your I-System is switched off, your naturally expanded awareness and wisdom will guide your behavior in all your activities of daily living. The expert in your life is sitting in your chair right here, right now.

In this chapter you will see how your natural emotions get captured by the I-System, and how you can take charge of your emotional life again with your true self in the driver's seat. You will also learn an advanced mapping practice called bubble mapping. This simple and effective tool gives you the ability to discover additional requirements that are activating your I-System while mapping. When your I-System is at rest, your emotions naturally regulate and your inner world becomes your friend. Reducing the activity of your I-System in the activities of daily living heals your addiction.

EMOTIONS: ASSETS OR LIABILITIES

1. Do an Emotion map. In the oval, write the emotion that's causing you the most difficulties in your life (for example, *worry, sadness, guilt, jealousy, love, joy,* or *happiness*). Around the oval, write your thoughts for a couple of minutes, without editing them.

EMOTION MAP

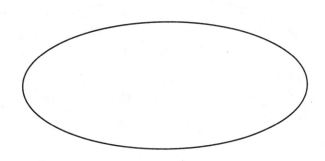

A. Mull over each item. Under each one, write your associated body tension and storylines.

B. Place a "D" next to each item that has depressor activity, and an "F" next to each item that has fixer activity. For example, if the item *I'll never be okay* has a lot of negative storylines and your body feels weighed down, it has depressor activity. If the item *She can't speak to me that way* has a lot of pressure-driven storylines like *What is she thinking? What is she doing?* and your body feels worked up and tense, the item has fixer activity.

C. How do you feel and act in this state?

_____

D. Is your I-System on or off? _____ If it's on, rate your I-System activity from 1 to 10: _____

Whenever an emotion is associated with pressure-driven storylines and an overly worked-up or slowed-down body, that emotion has been captured by the I-System.

2. Do the map again, writing the same emotion in the oval. Before you start writing, listen to background sounds and feel your body's pressure on your seat, your feet on the floor, and the pen in your hand. Take your time. Once you are settled, keep feeling the pen in your hand as you start writing. Watch the ink go onto the paper, and listen to background sounds. For the next few minutes, jot down any thoughts that come to mind.

EMOTION MAP WITH BRIDGING

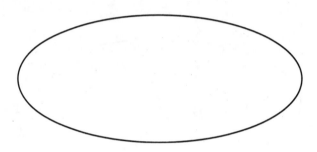

A. How does your body feel, and how do you act in this state?

_____

_____

B. Is your I-System on or off? _____   If it's on, rate your I-System activity from 1 to 10: _____

The emotions on this map, which are not associated with body tension, come from your true self.

Every single emotion you will ever experience arises from your reservoir of natural functioning. When the I-System captures that emotion, it either adds on to it (such as making you so anxious that you can't sleep or take care of your responsibilities) or takes away from it (such as making you so numb that you are unable to take care of yourself or others).

During the day, whenever your emotions seem to be getting the best of you, use your bridging awareness practices and thought labeling to recognize the two parts of emotions: *thoughts* and *body sensations*. As you have learned from your bridging map, a calmer mind and body allow you to experience your emotions without your I-System creating additional problems. This puts your natural true self in the driver's seat. Try it right now. Recall an emotion-filled situation, listen to background sounds, and notice what happens to your body. As your body settles, your emotions become natural functioning and no longer overwhelm you.

WHO RUNS YOUR LIFE: YOU OR YOUR EMOTIONS?

When you are in charge of your emotions, you bring harmony and balance to your daily life. As long as your I-System is quiet, your true self is able to deal with the strongest emotions, such as anxiety, hate, greed, jealousy, shame, guilt, love, happiness, and joy. It's not about the quality or quantity of the emotion; it's simply about who's in charge: your limited, damaged self or your expansive, true self. No matter how deep your love is or how strong your other emotions are, if your I-System is in charge, it will taint how you experience and express your emotions.

1. List three experiences you had where positive emotions caused you to make poor decisions and not take good care of yourself.

Experience	Positive Emotion
Fell in love, would text her day and night, and worried all day if she didn't text me right back.	Love

2. List three experiences you had where negative emotions caused you to make poor decisions and not take good care of yourself.

Experience	Negative Emotion
Had an argument with a colleague, said some nasty things that put a strain on our working relationship.	Anger

POSITIVE EMOTIONAL EXPERIENCE

1. From your prior list, select the positive emotion that resulted in the most distress and write it in the oval. Take a couple of minutes to write your thoughts around the oval. Work quickly without editing your thoughts.

STRONGEST POSITIVE EMOTION MAP

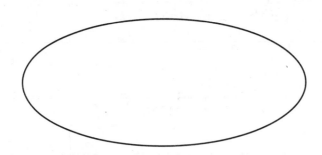

A. Mull over each item. Under each one, write your associated body tension and storylines.

B. Place a "D" next to each item that has depressor activity, and an "F" next to each item that has fixer activity.

C. What are your requirements?

_____

_____

_____

D. Is your I-System on or off? _____   If it's on, rate your I-System activity from 1 to 10: _____

2. Do this map again. Write the same positive emotion in the oval. Before you continue writing, listen to any background sounds, feel your body's pressure on your seat, sense your feet on the floor, and feel the pen in your hand. Take your time. Once you feel settled, keep feeling the pen in your hand and start writing. Watch the ink go onto the paper, and listen to any background sounds. For the next few minutes, jot down whatever thoughts pop into your mind.

STRONGEST POSITIVE EMOTION MAP WITH BRIDGING

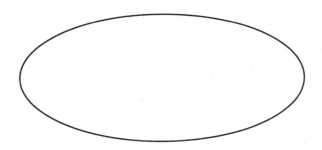

A. What are the differences between the two maps?

_____

_____

B. What recovery tools will you use to defuse the rest of your requirements on the first map in the exercise?

_____

C. Is your I-System on or off? _____ If it's on, rate your I-System activity from 1 to 10: _____

D. Do you see how your I-System causes your distress, not your emotions? Yes _____ No _____

When an intense emotion arises, it is important to recognize if your true self is experiencing it, or if the I-System's fixer or depressor are involved. If the emotion has been grabbed by the I-System, listen to the background sounds, label your thoughts, and recognize your storylines. It's also helpful to map out your requirements connected to this captured emotion. Switching off the I-System lets each emotion return to natural functioning. When requirements have been recognized, your I-System quiets and all your emotions, both positive and negative, are natural functioning. Your addiction heals.

139

NEGATIVE EMOTIONAL EXPERIENCE

1. From the earlier list, select the negative emotion that caused you the most anxiety and write it in the oval. Write your thoughts around the oval for a couple of minutes.

STRONGEST NEGATIVE EMOTION MAP

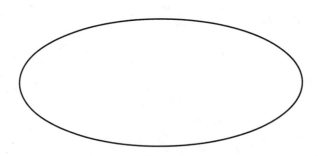

A. Mull over each item. Under each one, write your associated body tension and storylines.

B. Place a "D" next to each item that has depressor activity, and an "F" next to each item that has fixer activity.

C. What are your requirements?

_____

_____

D. Is your I-System on or off? _____ If it's on, rate your I-System activity from 1 to 10: _____

2. Do this map again. Write the same negative emotion in the oval. Before you continue writing, use your bridging awareness practices. Listen to background sounds and feel your body's pressure on your seat, your feet on the floor, and the pen in your hand. Take your time. Once you are settled, keep feeling the pen in your hand as you start writing. Watch the ink go onto the paper, and listen to background sounds. For the next few minutes, jot down any thoughts that come to mind.

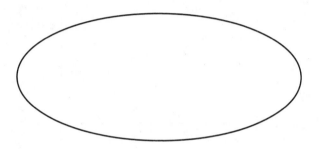

STRONGEST NEGATIVE EMOTION MAP WITH BRIDGING

A. What are the differences between the two maps?

_____

_____

B. Is your I-System or your powerful self in charge?

_____

C. What recovery tools will you use to defuse the remaining requirements on the first map in the exercise?

_____

_____

D. Is your I-System on or off? _____ If it's on, rate your I-System activity from 1 to 10: _____

E. Do you see how your I-System causes your distress, not your emotions? Yes _____ No _____

As this map shows, your negative emotions are not your enemy. When you are in natural functioning, you experience your emotions without additional distress. Your true self automatically results in mind-body well-being. Your addiction heals.

STAY CALM IN A CRISIS

1. We have all had situations where we felt comfortable that everything was under control and then something suddenly happened that caused a crisis that could set us up for a relapse. Fill out the chart below, and list some of those situations.

Troubling Situation	Your Reaction	Requirement
Having to go to my brother-in-law's house for dinner.	Argue with my wife about why we have to go. Get angry.	I shouldn't have to go to his house. My wife shouldn't have arranged for us to go.

It's crucial to be aware of when you see the first signs of an active I-System. When you use your recovery tools right away, you stop your I-System from taking control and prevent overwhelming emotions, urges, and cravings.

2. From the prior chart, choose the most troubling situation that created the most distress. Write that situation in the oval. Around the oval, write your thoughts for a couple of minutes without editing them.

CRISIS MAP

A. What is your body tension and how does it progress?

_____

B. List your depressor/fixer storylines:

_____

_____

_____

C. Look at your map again. Draw a circle (bubble) around the thought that has the *most* body tension. Take a few minutes to write your thoughts around that bubbled item. "Bubble" mapping helps you uncover more of your requirements. Bubble map other troubling thoughts on this map.

D. Identify and list as many requirements as you can:

_____

_____

_____

143

3. Do the map again, writing the same troubling situation in the oval. Before you continue writing, listen to background sounds and feel your body's pressure on your seat, your feet on the floor, and the pen in your hand. Take your time. Once you are settled, keep feeling the pen in your hand as you start writing. Watch the ink go onto the paper, and listen to background sounds. For the next few minutes, jot down any thoughts that come to mind.

CRISIS MAP WITH BRIDGING

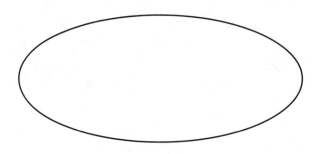

A. What's your mind-body state after bridging, and how do you act in this state?

_____

_____

B. How did your attempt to defuse your remaining requirements go?

_____

_____

Remember, for those requirements that are hard to defuse, find and break down the large requirement into smaller ones. For example, take the requirement *She should love me.* You know what your requirement is, but you're having trouble defusing it. So ask yourself, *What does that requirement look like?* For example: *She should smile when she sees me, She shouldn't get angry with me, She should not criticize me, She should always compliment me.* These more detailed requirements are easier to work with and defuse. When you defuse them, the requirement that was hard to defuse (*She should love me*) will defuse on its own.

FEAR

1. Throughout the day, notice the events (for example, *My coworker was fired* or *I'm going to propose*) that led you to become fearful. Recognize the underlying requirement (*I shouldn't lose my job, She should say yes*).

Event	Fear	Requirement
Coworker was fired.	I could be fired next.	I shouldn't lose my job.
Marriage proposal.	I'll mess it up, She'll say no.	She should say yes.
I recognized a problem at work and have a solution.	I might look stupid if I don't say it right.	I should be able to present it clearly. They should adopt my solution.

2. Think back over the past month and list the three greatest fears that caused you distress. Find and list the hidden requirements for each:

_____

_____

_____

3. Do a Fear map, writing your greatest fear in the oval. Write your thoughts around the oval for a couple of minutes without editing them.

FEAR MAP

A. Note the body tension associated with each item and draw a bubble around the thought that brings the most body tension. Take a few minutes to scatter more thoughts around the bubbled item. Bubble map any other troubling items.

B. List your depressor/fixer storylines:

_____

_____

C. Identify and list as many requirements as you can:

_____

_____

_____

D. Is your I-System on or off? _____ If it's on, rate your I-System activity from 1 to 10: _____

Fear is a natural emotion from executive functioning that alerts you to possible danger. Remember that fear, like other emotions, has two parts: a thought and a body sensation. When the I-System captures your fear, it convinces you that you can't cope and fills you with paralyzing distress, making you a victim of your fear. Fighting fear never works because your depressor/fixer takes over and creates even more distress and impaired ability to respond to the situation.

4. Do this map again, writing the same fear in the oval. Before you start writing, listen to background sounds and feel your body's pressure on your seat, your feet on the floor, and the pen in your hand. Take your time. Once you are settled, keep feeling the pen in your hand as you start writing. Watch the ink go onto the paper, and listen to background sounds. For the next few minutes, jot down any thoughts that come to mind.

FEAR MAP WITH BRIDGING

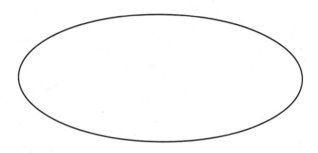

A. What's your mind-body state on this map, compared to the previous one?

_____

_____

B. How would you act differently in this state?

_____

_____

C. Is your I-System on or off? _____ If it's on, rate your I-System activity from 1 to 10: _____

D. Do you think you can defuse your requirements from the previous map the next time the situation comes up? Yes _____ No _____

In mind-body bridging, being fearless doesn't mean you have no fear. Fear is a natural emotion from executive functioning. Being fearless means that your I-System has not paralyzed your natural ability to deal with the situation that evoked the fear. To control the I-System's influence on your fear, defuse the underlying requirements. When you defuse requirements, rather than reacting to a fearful situation, you deal with the situation with your true self in charge. This heals your addiction.

BEFRIEND YOUR GREATEST DREAD

1. Having a solid foundation of mind-body bridging, let's befriend your greatest dread. Before you do this advanced map, be in a quiet place where you can have fifteen minutes of uninterrupted time. Take a while to consider what your greatest dread is. Write that dread in the oval. Write your thoughts around the oval. Take your time. Describe your body tension at the bottom of the map.

> ## GREATEST DREAD MAP

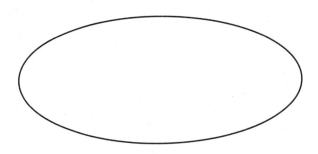

Body Tension: _____

A. Is your I-System on or off? _____ If it's on, rate your I-System activity from 1 to 10: _____

B. Looking at your map, list the signs of your active I-System (requirements, depressor/fixer, storylines):

_____

_____

_____

C. Take the next five to ten minutes to befriend your map. To do that, listen to background sounds and feel your body's pressure on your seat, your feet on the floor, and the pen in your hand. When you become settled, go over each item on your map gently and kindly until your mind and body do not overreact to the item. If an item causes tension, use thought labeling. When you can review your entire map without body tension or anxiety, your map has been befriended. Your mind is not your enemy!

2. Do this map again, writing the same thing in the oval. Before you start writing, use your bridging awareness practices. Listen to background sounds and feel your body's pressure on your seat, your feet on the floor, and the pen in your hand. Take your time. Once you are settled, keep feeling the pen in your hand as you start writing. Watch the ink go onto the paper, and listen to background sounds. For the next few minutes, jot down any thoughts that come to mind.

GREATEST DREAD MAP WITH BRIDGING

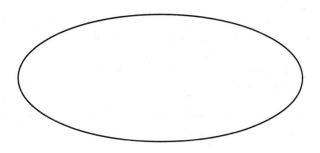

A. What do you notice that's different on this map?

_____

_____

B. When the requirements on your previous map come up again in your life, how are you going to defuse them?

_____

_____

C. Does your greatest dread in the oval still create body tension and mental distress and disconnect you from your true self?   Yes _____   No _____

D. Is your true self always within you, no matter what?   Yes _____   No _____

E. For other remaining overwhelming emotions, repeat this two-part map until you have befriended those emotions as well.

AWARENESS TOOLS TO BEFRIEND EMOTIONS

Thinking, body sensations, and all emotions are only problems when your I-System is active. Emotions, cravings, and urges are not your enemies! But when you push them away, deny them, or declare a state of war with them, it only reinforces the I-System's control. When you befriend painful thoughts, body sensations, and emotions, a natural healing process begins to take place.

Here are the powerful awareness tools to befriend your emotions.

1. In any situation, become aware of the early signs of an active I-System—unpleasantly stirred up body sensations, mental urgency, and spinning negative storylines—and recognize when your depressor/fixer is beginning to take control.

2. Use bridging awareness practices and thought labeling to calm down your I-System.

3. Use your true self's awareness to notice any stories that the fixer or depressor may spin. These storylines impair your ability to act, and add even more distress.

4. Without judging, gently and patiently uncover the depressor activity that is reinforcing your unpleasant body sensations and negative feelings about yourself.

5. Open your awareness to all of your sights, sounds, and body sensations as well as your emotions. This awareness prevents your I-System from taking control.

6. Recognize and defuse the requirements that activate your addicted mode and I-System. (Mapping helps.)

7. Be aware that it's not the activity you are doing but who's doing it that is important. If it is your I-System's damaged self, you will remain prone to entering into an addicted mode. If it's your true self, in a natural functioning state, you will heal from your addiction.

Thinking, body sensations, and emotions are a natural part of life. When you become aware that an emotion has been captured by the I-System, you have a choice to make: use and embrace the emotion as an ally that signals to you that your I-System is switched on, or reject the information and let your I-System be in control. Your natural self accepts "you" without judging whether you or the emotion are good or bad, friend or foe. This nonjudgmental awareness automatically switches off your I-System and stops the problematic emotion in its tracks. When you befriend the urges and cravings of your addicted mode by expanding your awareness and defusing your requirements, the unsettling symptoms lose their power over you. This state of expanded awareness means that your I-System is not active. Your true self in a natural functioning state, with all its healing abilities, creates a balanced mind-body state that allows you to live your best life.

RESTORING NATURAL EMOTIONS

Whenever your emotions make you feel unsettled or overwhelmed, know that it's not "just you." It's your I-System that has taken over your natural emotion and caused your turmoil. It's important to see how the depressor and fixer affect your natural emotions. When the depressor is interfering with your emotion, it is usually easier to recognize because of the negative storylines and the heavy, unpleasant feeling in your body. However, if the fixer is responsible, it's not always as easy to recognize because the fixer tries to mask over the unpleasant thoughts and body sensations. The following are some examples of how the fixer works.

A. It takes your natural emotion of jealousy, which is originally a signal for you to pay attention to your relationship, and converts it to an out-of-control preoccupation. Because the fixer justifies this unhealthy emotion and behavior with storylines, it is more difficult to recognize. Even if your story is accurate, the fact that it's a storyline means that your I-System has greatly limited your ability to deal with the situation.

B. The fixer takes your natural emotion of anxiety, which in its untainted state signals you to pay attention to something that is going on in your life, and revs it up into a panic-filled state. Because the fixer has your mind and body so wound up and disturbed, you feel and act as if a panic reaction is your only choice. When the I-System is quiet, the natural emotion of anxiety enters your expanded awareness. Your naturally functioning true self acknowledges the signal and deals appropriately with it.

C. Cravings can also be broken down into thoughts and body sensations. When the I-System is active, cravings become impelling thoughts and compelling body sensations where you feel using is your only choice. When the I-System is quiet, those pushy thoughts and prodding body sensations enter your expanded awareness and your true self, in natural functioning, acknowledges the signal and deals appropriately with them.

D. Lastly, when your natural emotion of happiness becomes filled with fears of losing that pleasant state, it's the fixer making you believe that happiness should last forever.

Once you become aware of how the depressor and fixer are taking over, know that your emotion has become tied to a requirement. When you realize there is an underlying requirement (*I should be able to talk comfortably in front of a group, I should be perfect*), the power of the I-System is automatically reduced. By recognizing and defusing the requirement (mapping helps), your emotions become appropriate and your shift into natural functioning prepares you to deal with the situation as it is without igniting your addicted mode. Every time you reduce the activity of the I-System in your usual activities of daily living, you greatly increase your capacity to handle strong emotions whenever and wherever they arise. Restoring natural emotions and healing your addiction go hand in hand.

REVIEW

Discover

- That a natural emotion has been captured by your I-System.

- How your I-System causes your emotions to get out of control.

- That uncontrolled emotions create relapses.

- That when your I-System is at rest, your emotions naturally regulate.

Experience

- Your emotions are not your enemy.

- Your innate power to restore natural emotions.

Apply

- Use bubble mapping to discover additional requirements that are activating your I-System.

- Know that all emotions (including cravings) are natural. Recognize that whenever emotions get out of hand, it's always due to a requirement that you are currently unaware of. The depressor and fixer have added on to or taken away from your natural emotions. Storylines keep the process going by fueling the I-System. When you expand your awareness in a non-judgmental way to recognize your I-System's activity, the I-System begins to lose its power, allowing your emotions to return to their natural state (natural functioning). You are now able to experience and express your natural emotions in a way that is best for you and the world, with your powerful self in charge.

Recovery tools

- Expand your awareness to recognize signs of emotions taken over by the I-System.

- Use nonjudgmental awareness to calm your I-System and restore your natural emotions.

- Bubble map the troubling items (thoughts associated with excess body tension) when your requirements are unclear.

- Befriend your emotions.

MBB RATING SCALE: TAKING CHARGE OF YOUR EMOTIONS

Date: _____

After using the tools in this chapter for several days, check the description that best matches your practice: hardly ever, sometimes, usually, or almost always.

How often do you...	Hardly Ever	Sometimes	Usually	Almost Always
Notice when your I-System has captured your emotions?				
Recognize the requirement driving the emotion?				
Bubble your maps to uncover additional requirements?				
Defuse requirements associated with emotions?				
Notice your active I-System creating your distress?				
Notice when your emotions are from your true self?				
Befriend your negative emotions?				

List three emotions that were captured by the I-System:

_____

_____

_____

What were the requirements?

_____

_____

_____

How did you befriend your emotions?

_____

_____

CHAPTER 8

ACHIEVE LASTING RECOVERY AND LIVE YOUR BEST LIFE

Discover, Experience, and Apply

Discover how the I-System interferes with your recovery.

Experience how defusing requirements solidifies your recovery.

Apply the recovery tools in your daily life to reduce the activity of your I-System and heal your addiction.

Mind-Body Language

Recovery action steps: Actions you take to achieve a recovery goal that come from the two-part mind-body mapping process, and are carried out by your naturally functioning true self.

WHO'S IN CHARGE OF YOUR RECOVERY?

As you have experienced in this mind-body workbook, any activity can be either I-System-driven or mediated through natural functioning. What is of primary importance is not only *what* you are doing, but *who* is doing it—your I-System-driven *damaged self* or your naturally functioning *true self*. The same applies to your recovery program. A recovery program driven by an active I-System has the same goal as addiction: to fix yourself. As with any addicted mode, you will continuously measure yourself against unattainable and perfectionist requirements. Instead of improving your well-being, this adds to your distress and feelings of inadequacy. Your fixer-captured thoughts and practices will drive you relentlessly to prove to others and yourself that you are okay, and your depressor will let you know that whatever you did was not good enough. Your recovery program can consist of healthy practices which are done to the utmost, but if they are done with an active I-System, it will compromise or could even have a destructive effect on your recovery and well-being.

12-step programs place a strong emphasis on the development of certain attitudes toward existence, referred to as spiritual principles (Du Plessis 2015). Although mind-body bridging and 12-step programs have fundamentally the same aim, mind-body bridging is not about cultivating any particular attitude. You are not broken and do not have to push yourself to adopt any spiritual attitude. Mind-body bridging simply focuses on quieting the I-System so that whatever attitude you display will be from your natural functioning's wellspring of healing, goodness, and wisdom. As you continue using your recovery tools to reduce the activity of your I-System in your daily life, compassion, kindness, and willingness to help others will naturally flow from within, without effort. With a resting I-System, your wellspring of healing, goodness, and wisdom flourishes. Mind-body bridging can assist those in 12-step programs to add these powerful recovery tools to their existing programs. It will help the process of moving from a life driven by the isolated and damaged self, which the I-System causes us to falsely believe, to a life lived from the true self that is connected to the source of goodness, well-being, and wisdom.

This chapter gives you the chance to put your true self in charge of your recovery, as you uncover even more requirements. Also, you will learn an effective new tool called *recovery action steps*. You use the two-part mapping process to find actions you may take to reach recovery goals that are free from interference of your I-System. When your I-System is at rest, you are in a natural functioning state, where you can achieve wellness and take care of yourself and your tasks without your addicted mode limiting your choices. This chapter brings together all your recovery tools so that you can effectively handle any challenge that comes up in life, without having to revert to substance abuse. Also in this chapter, you will learn an advanced, rapid-fire mapping practice to find your stubbornly hidden requirements, called *power mapping*. This free-association tool quickly expands your awareness of your requirements about a problem, situation, event, or person that is causing you distress. Without using your bridging awareness practices, you do map after map, just watching your switched-on I-System in action. When you power map, your I-System has free rein, but at the same time, your true self is still in the driver's seat. When you make a habit of power mapping, you experience firsthand that no matter what happens, your powerful true self remains in charge.

The future is often uncertain and unpredictable. No one has control over what the future has in store for us. What you do have control over is who is in charge, your damaged self or your true self.

WHO ARE YOU?

Do a Who Am I? map. Inside the circle, write the qualities that best describe who you are. After you have listed at least six qualities, outside the circle write the opposite of each quality, and connect it with a line. If needed, see the sample map that follows.

WHO AM I? MAP

SAMPLE MAP: WHO AM I?

1. How does each quality *inside* the circle make you feel? Describe your body tension:

    _____

    _____

2. How does each quality *outside* the circle make you feel? Describe your body tension:

    _____

    _____

    _____

3. Do the qualities inside the circle *really* describe who you are?   Yes _____   No _____

4. Do the qualities outside the circle *really* describe who you are?   Yes _____   No _____

Your I-System has you believing that the qualities inside the circle define you. Whenever you think you have any of the qualities outside the circle, your I-System tells you that you're lacking or damaged. Your actions then follow that feeling state. Your I-System wants to convince you that you are who you *think* you are. The qualities you listed are just thoughts about you, not you.

5. Each quality inside the circle has become a requirement if the opposite quality outside the circle has body tension or a negative emotional reaction. List your requirements:

    _____

    _____

    _____

    _____

    _____

    _____

    _____

When you use your recovery tools to rest your I-System, you automatically expand the circle to include everything on your map. When you aren't driven by your requirements, you are *everything*, which means you can have any quality on your map (even negative ones) without activating your I-System. When your true self is in charge, who you are is no longer limited by your I-System. Who you are is so vast, boundless, and ever changing that your thinking mind can't grasp it. You are much greater than who you think you are. In this state of harmony and balance, you make the right choices to take care of yourself. Your recovery therefore does not need to be driven by an attempt to fix the negative qualities or force the adoption of positive qualities.

DO YOUR QUALITIES DEFINE OR CONFINE YOU?

Take a couple of minutes to think about your five most important qualities. Write one of your five most important qualities (for example, *trustworthy, hardworking,* or *intelligent*) inside each of the sections of the circle below. One or two words will do for each quality.

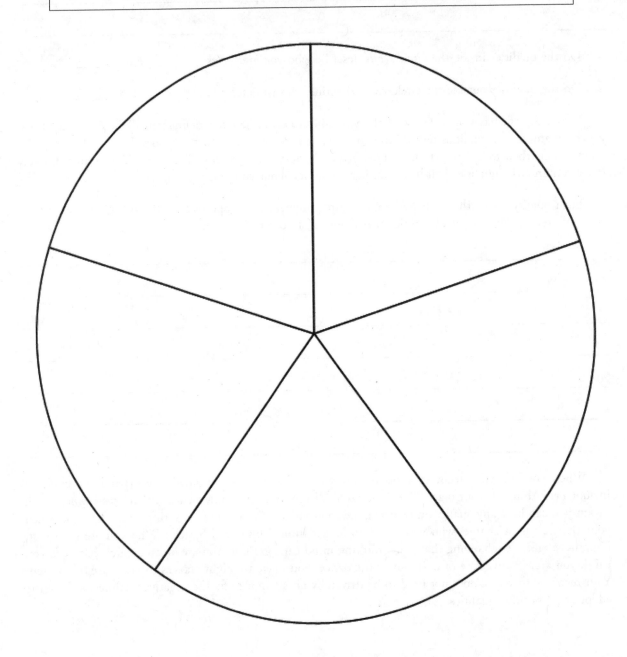

MY FIVE MOST IMPORTANT QUALITIES MAP

1. Look at your map and cross out the quality that's least important to you. What's your reaction as you imagine yourself without this first quality?

_____

_____

2. Cross out the quality that's the next least important to you. What's your reaction as you imagine yourself without this second quality?

_____

_____

3. Again, cross out the quality that's the next least important to you. What's your reaction as you cross out this third quality?

_____

_____

4. Choose between the last two qualities on your map and cross out the one that's less important to you. What's your reaction when you cross out this next-to-last quality?

_____

_____

5. Think about the last remaining quality. Cross it out. What's your experience now?

_____

_____

The levels of mental distress and body tension, and how hard it is to cross out these naturally functioning qualities, show how strongly the I-System confines you. It takes hold of your qualities and turns them into requirements. It's as if your goodness depends on meeting those requirements. Your reaction and body sensations when you were crossing out your qualities show how strongly your I-System tries to define you as a limited set of qualities.

As long as you have these self-limiting requirements, your recovery will be filled with disappointment. This is bound to happen because you will never be able to satisfy your I-System requirements. Whenever one of these requirements is not met, you will melt down. With a calm I-System, your natural true self is no longer confined to a narrow way of seeing yourself.

HOPES AND FEARS

1. Do a Hopes and Fears map. Take a couple of minutes to write around the oval whatever hopes and fears pop into your mind. Describe your body tension at the bottom of the map.

HOPES AND FEARS MAP

HOPES AND FEARS

Body Tension: _____

A. Is your I-System on or off? _____   If it's on, rate your I-System activity from 1 to 10: _____

B. Looking at your map, list the signs of your active I-System (requirements, depressor/fixer, storylines):

_____

_____

C. How would you feel and act in this mind-body state?

_____

_____

D. How would your reaction affect your recovery?

_____

_____

2. Do this map again. Before you start writing, use your bridging awareness practices. Listen to background sounds and feel your body's pressure on your seat, your feet on the floor, and the pen in your hand. Take your time. Once you are settled, keep feeling the pen in your hand as you start writing. Watch the ink go onto the paper, and listen to background sounds. For the next few minutes, jot down any thoughts that come to mind about your hopes and fears.

HOPES AND FEARS MAP WITH BRIDGING

A. What do you notice that's different on this map?

_____

_____

B. Defuse the requirements on your previous map. How did it go?

_____

_____

C. Do the fearful items on the previous map still create anxiety and impair your ability to care for yourself? Yes _____ No _____

D. If your answer is yes, go back and use your bridging awareness practices and thought labeling on each of the items that still cause you problems.

E. Is your true self always with you, no matter what? Yes _____ No _____

WHAT'S STILL HOLDING YOU BACK FROM ACHIEVING YOUR RECOVERY GOALS?

1. List the biggest things holding you back from achieving your recovery goals. Do they include your genes, background, lack of discipline or self-control, trauma, or something else?

   _____

2. Do a What's Holding Me Back map. In the oval, write the biggest thing that's holding you back. Around the oval, write your thoughts for a couple of minutes without editing them. Describe your body tension at the bottom of the map.

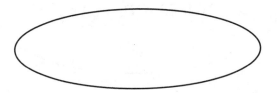

WHAT'S HOLDING ME BACK MAP

Body Tension: _____

A. List your depressor/fixer storylines:

   _____

   _____

B. List your requirements:

   _____

   _____

C. Bubble your map, drawing a bubble around a thought that has a lot of body tension. Take a few minutes to write more thoughts around the bubbled item. Bubble any other troubling items to help you identify your health and wellness requirements.

   It's not the item listed above that's holding you back from your recovery goals; it's the I-System, which has taken these items (*No self-control*) and created requirements (*I should have self-control*). Once self-control is a requirement, whatever you do will activate your I-System and the depressor/fixer cycle will beat you up. Defusing your requirements automatically connects you to your innate powers of self-control where your natural functioning is unleashed.

3. Do this map again. In the oval, write the same problem that's holding you back. Before you start writing, listen to background sounds and feel your body's pressure on your seat, your feet on the floor, and the pen in your hand. Take your time. Once you are settled, keep feeling the pen in your hand as you start writing. Watch the ink go onto the paper, and listen to background sounds. For the next few minutes, jot down any thoughts that come to mind.

WHAT'S HOLDING ME BACK MAP WITH BRIDGING

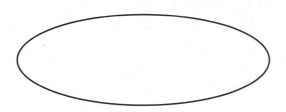

A. How is this map different from the prior map?

_____

B. What is really holding you back?

_____

C. Is your I-System on or off? _____ If it's on, rate your I-System activity from 1 to 10: _____

D. Can you see that even if you have a serious disease, it is only your I-System that is holding you back from accessing your healing powers? Yes _____ No _____

Accessing your innate power to live your best life is what recovery is about and can only be done by reducing the activity of your I-System in your daily life.

OVERTHINKING IMPAIRS YOUR RECOVERY

One of the most common mental states that prevent many recovering addicts from reaching their recovery goals is overthinking.

1. List five situations where your over-thinking bogs you down, leading to addiction symptoms. Find the requirement behind each event.

Situation	Overthinking	Requirement
Can't sleep the night before giving a presentation.	I can't stop going over and over it. I'm making myself anxious and can't get to sleep.	I should give a perfect presentation, I should be able to sleep.
Can't get over how thoughtless and mean he was.	I'm like a broken record and keep going over and over again what he did, why I think he did it, and what it might mean.	He should be thoughtful and kind.

The first step in dealing with a situation that is causing you to move into an addicted mode and bogging you down is to notice that over-thinking is a signal that your I-System is on. Note your body tension—for example, tight shoulders or a knot in your stomach. Next, use your favorite bridging awareness practice (such as listening to background sounds or rubbing your fingers together) and find your requirement. To defuse a requirement, remember to recognize that it's not the situation or even your overthinking that is creating your distress; it's your I-System's requirement. Some requirements are easy to defuse, but if the requirement is hard to defuse, there may be other, related requirements you haven't found yet. Doing maps like the following ones will help.

2. Map the most troubling situation from the prior list where thinking too much has bogged you down. Write that situation in the oval (for example, *People disrespecting me*). Around the oval, write your thoughts for a couple of minutes without editing them. Describe your body tension at the bottom of the map.

OVERTHINKING MAP

Body Tension: _____

A. What are your depressor/fixer?

_____

_____

B. Find and list your hidden requirements.

_____

_____

C. Bubble your map, drawing a bubble around an item that has a lot of body tension. Take a few minutes to write more thoughts around the bubbled item. Bubble any other items filled with body tension to help you find hidden requirements.

3. Do the previous map again, writing the same situation in the oval. Before you start writing, listen to background sounds and feel your body's pressure on your seat, your feet on the floor, and the pen in your hand. Take your time. Once you are settled, keep feeling the pen in your hand as you start writing. Watch the ink go onto the paper, and listen to background sounds. For the next few minutes, jot down any thoughts that come to mind.

OVERTHINKING MAP WITH BRIDGING

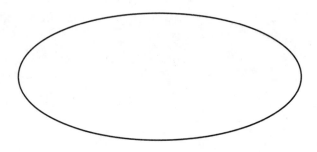

A. What's your mind-body state on this map, compared to the previous map?

_____

_____

B. How would you feel and act differently if you were in this state?

_____

_____

C. Do you see that the real problem is not your thinking, but your I-System being turned on by requirements and driving your storylines?   Yes _____   No _____

D. Describe how you will recognize and defuse your requirements in real time:

_____

_____

WHEN IS ENOUGH NOT ENOUGH?

Our I-System keeps comparing us to others. By creating requirements about how we and the world should be, it tells us that we don't have enough of *something* (money, smarts, looks, education, or recovery), resulting in excess worry, fear, and resentment.

1. Think about a situation where you didn't have enough time, money, energy, attractiveness, self-discipline, talent, and so on that still brings up body tension and mind clutter. Now fill out the chart below.

Situation	Your Reaction	Requirements
Didn't have enough time to study for final exam.	Got anxious; dropped the course.	I should have more time to study. I should be more prepared.
Upcoming job interview.	Couldn't sleep for days. Worried that they won't hire me. Uptight with anticipation.	I shouldn't have to interview. I should be acceptable. I should not be so uptight. They should hire me.
Getting ready for a first date.	Couldn't decide what to wear. Anxious if she will like me. Stomachache, worried all day.	I should look perfect. I should be at my best. She should like me.

As long as your requirements are not defused, your I-System will control your life and create anxiety and jealousy. It is not what the other person has or what he or she is doing that is causing your difficulties; it's your I-System making you feel you will never have enough. The following maps will clarify the situation for you.

2. From the previous chart, choose the most distressing situation and write it in the oval below. Next, around the oval, write your thoughts about the situation. Write for a couple of minutes.

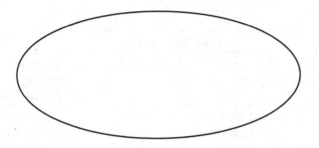

NOT ENOUGH MAP

A. What is your body tension and how does it progress?

_____

B. What are your depressors?

_____

C. What are your fixers?

_____

D. What are your storylines?

_____

E. List your requirements:

_____

_____

F. Bubble your map, drawing a bubble around a thought that has a lot of body tension. Take a few minutes to write more thoughts around the bubbled item. Bubble any other items filled with addiction symptoms to help you find any hidden requirements.

3. Do this map again using bridging awareness practices. Write the same distressing situation in the oval. Before you continue writing, listen to background sounds and feel your body's pressure on your seat, your feet on the floor, and the pen in your hand. Take your time. Once you are settled, keep feeling the pen in your hand as you start writing. Watch the ink go onto the paper, and keep listening to background sounds. For the next few minutes, jot down any thoughts that come to mind about the situation.

NOT ENOUGH MAP WITH BRIDGING

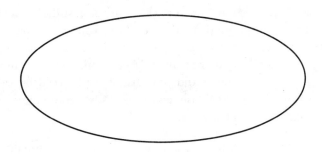

A. What do you notice that is different on this map?

_____

B. How do you act when your I-System is switched off?

_____

C. How will you defuse your requirements on the previous map when the situation arises again?

_____

_____

After doing the bridging map, if you still have body tension and feel you may have a hard time when the situation comes up again, use the following information about power mapping to find those stubbornly hidden requirements. Power mapping is only for people who have had success with using mind-body bridging practices in their daily lives. Use power mapping when your active I-System is hard to handle.

POWER MAP YOUR WAY OUT OF HARD-TO-DEFUSE REQUIREMENTS

Power mapping is an advanced tool that only works when you have a solid foundation of mind-body bridging practices and have had success in recognizing and defusing requirements. It is important to have at least twenty to thirty minutes of time to yourself when you power map.

1. To power map, sit down with a pen and pad of paper. In the center of the paper, write the issue that troubles you the most (for example, "I don't have enough money to pay my bills"). Draw an oval around that issue and quickly jot down whatever thoughts come to mind. Let your I-System run wild as you write. Don't use your bridging awareness practices, don't try to reduce your distress, and don't try to solve the issue. All you have to do is watch your I-System in action. When you have completed the map, write down your body tension at the bottom of the page.

2. Now take the most distressing thought from the map you just did, write it in an oval on another piece of paper, and begin mapping that thought. When you finish, write down your body tension at the bottom of the page. Repeat this process by taking the most distressing thought on one map and making it the topic of the next map. Make map after map after map. Map for as long as it takes, until your I-System quiets and your distress naturally decreases. Look over your maps for requirements you were not previously aware of. Those requirements were switching on your I-System and fueling your addicted mode.

3. Review your series of maps and note how your body tension eventually reduces as your mental distress quiets down. It's not possible to have mental distress without body tension.

When you power map, your I-System is on, but your true self remains in charge as you keep mapping. Let your I-System run free as you jot down your thoughts, emotions, and body tension. As time goes on, you will see that your I-System will, over time, run out of steam as you keep mapping. You are finding your hidden requirements while exhausting your I-System. This shows you that you can deal with mental pressures, and body tension, without having to revert to substance abuse or destructive behaviors.

How did it go?

_____

_____

_____

We all have an I-System and will never be rid of it. It's there to remind you of when you are off course (figure 2.1), when your damaged self is active. It's your friend and your compass, telling you that you are not in a natural functioning state. Power mapping shows you that no matter how intense your I-System is, you can always be the boss of your I-System.

NOW IS THE ONLY TIME YOU CAN TAKE CARE OF YOURSELF

1. Do a Past, Present, and Future map. In the "Past" section of this map, take a couple of minutes to jot down whatever comes to mind about your past. Then describe your body tension. Next, in the "Future" section of this map, take another couple of minutes to write whatever comes to mind about your future. Describe your body tension. Finally, in the "Present" section of this map, take a couple of minutes to jot down whatever comes to mind about the present and, again, describe your body tension.

PAST, PRESENT, AND FUTURE MAP

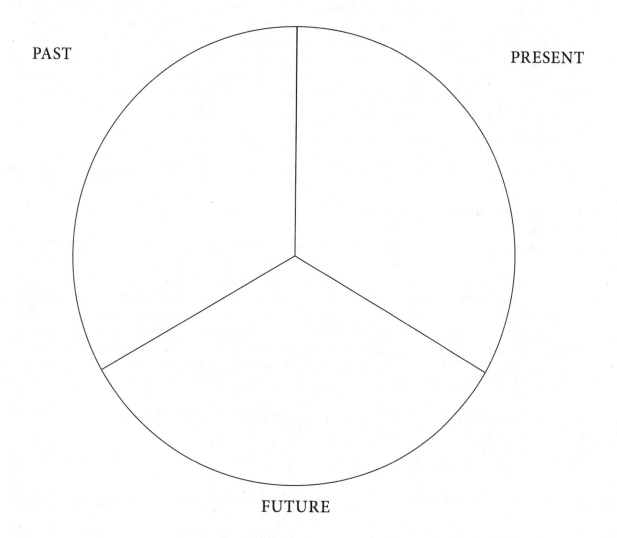

PAST

PRESENT

FUTURE

Let's think about this remarkable map.

A. The "Past" section of your map is full of storylines with themes like *My father was an alcoholic* and *My friends always pushed me to party*. True or not, positive or negative, these stories create mind clutter; they tense your body and take you away from the present. When you recognize storylines in real time, notice that they take you away from doing what you need to do in the present.

What do you notice about the "Past" section of your map? List your storylines:

_____

_____

_____

B. The "Future" section of your map may have many of your hopes and dreams. Beside each item that brings body tension, write the requirements you can find. For instance, if the item that's creating body tension is *I must lose weight*, the requirement is *I should be slim*. The I-System has taken hold of your naturally functioning thought, turned it into a requirement, and filled your body with tension and your mind with clutter. When thoughts about the future that are driven by the I-System come up in real time, note your body tension, find your requirements, and use bridging awareness practices and thought labeling to bring you back to the present.

List the requirements you notice on the "Future" section of your map:

_____

_____

_____

C. The "Present" section of this map shows what you currently feel and think. Look for signs of an active I-System, such as body tension, depressors, fixers, and storylines. Can you uncover your requirements? The I-System has taken stuff from your past and future to try to fix your damaged image of yourself. Look carefully for signs of the fixer and then find the hidden depressor. The depressor makes you feel broken and drives the fixer. You now know that the fixer can never "fix" the damage, because you aren't broken. You don't need fixing. The damaged self is caused by your active I-System, not what you have been through, and it limits your ability to recover and fully live in the present.

List any signs of an active I-System you find in the "Present" section of your map. Also list your depressors, fixers, storylines, and requirements:

_____

_____

_____

2. Do a Present map. Before you start writing about the present, use your bridging awareness practices. Listen to background sounds and feel your body's pressure on your seat, your feet on the floor, and the pen in your hand. Take your time. Once you are settled, keep feeling the pen in your hand as you start writing any thoughts that come to mind about the present. Watch the ink go onto the paper, and keep listening to background sounds.

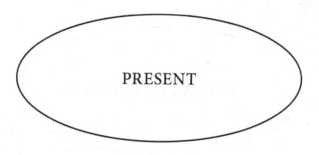

| PRESENT MAP WITH BRIDGING |

A. What do you notice about this map that's different from the "Present" section of your Past, Present, and Future Map?

_____

_____

B. Note how you would take care of yourself and your responsibilities in this mind-body state:

_____

_____

Being in the present is not being in a zone, nor is it a moment of enlightenment or a serene state of being. Your true self is always present right here, right now. When your I-System is calm, you are in the present, where your recovery is on course. Requirements take you away from your true self that is living right here, right now. If your depressor has you feeling *down, bored, overwhelmed, lacking,* or *hopeless,* you have a hidden requirement that's pulling you down. On the other hand, when your fixer has you feeling jittery and anxious, and as if *enough is never enough,* you have a hidden requirement that's also taking over your natural functioning. When your I-System is active, look for your hidden requirements and use bridging awareness practices to come back to the present moment, do what you need to do, and take care of yourself right now.

WHO'S IN CHARGE OF YOUR RECOVERY GOALS

Now let's see who is in charge of your recovery goals.

1. Around the oval, write some of your recovery goals (*Stay clean and sober, Repair relationships*) and your thoughts about them (*I have tried many times and always fail*). Write for a couple of minutes without editing your thoughts. Describe your body tension at the bottom of the map.

RECOVERY GOALS MAP

Body Tension: _____

A. Is your I-System on or off? _____   If it's on, rate your I-System activity from 1 to 10: _____

B. What are your depressors?

_____

C. What are your fixers?

_____

D. What are your storylines?

_____

E. What are your requirements?

_____

F. How do you achieve your recovery goals in this state?

_____

2. Do this map again using bridging awareness practices. Before you start writing about your recovery goals, listen to background sounds and feel your body's pressure on your seat, your feet on the floor, and the pen in your hand. Take your time. Once you are settled, keep feeling the pen in your hand as you start writing. Watch the ink go onto the paper, and keep listening to background sounds. For the next few minutes, jot down any thoughts that come to mind.

RECOVERY GOALS MAP WITH BRIDGING

RECOVERY GOALS

A. How is this map the same as or different from the previous map?

_____

B. Are any of the items associated with body tension?   Yes _____   No _____

C. For those items with body tension, do you recognize your requirements?

_____

_____

D. List the self-care goals that don't have associated body tension:

_____

_____

_____

To stop your I-System from influencing your recovery goals, simply quiet your I-System by defusing your requirements. This puts your natural self, rather than your I-System, in charge of your recovery.

DISCOVER YOUR RECOVERY ACTION STEPS

1. Select one of the recovery goals listed on your previous map that was free of body tension. Write it in the oval. Next, take a couple of minutes to write around the oval your thoughts about what you are going to do to achieve that goal. Be specific. Describe your body tension at the bottom of the map.

RECOVERY GOAL ACHIEVEMENT MAP

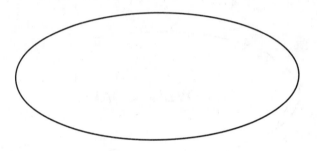

Body Tension: _____

A. What are your depressors?

_____

B. What are your fixers?

_____

C. What are your storylines?

_____

D. What are your requirements?

_____

_____

E. Is your I-System on or off? _____   If it's on, rate your I-System activity from 1 to 10: _____

Did you see how your I-System grabbed a recovery goal that used to be without body tension, created requirements about reaching your goal, and limited your success? Your active I-System will always muddle your path to recovery.

2. Do this map again using bridging awareness practices. Write the same goal in the oval. Before you start writing about how you are going to achieve that goal, listen to background sounds and feel your body's pressure on your seat, your feet on the floor, and the pen in your hand. Take your time. Once you are settled, keep feeling the pen in your hand as you start writing. Watch the ink go onto the paper, and keep listening to background sounds. Write for a couple of minutes.

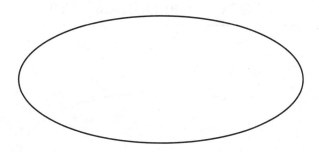

RECOVERY GOAL ACHIEVEMENT MAP WITH BRIDGING

A. Circle those items *without* body tension. These are possible action steps.

B. Choose three of these items as the *recovery action steps* you plan to take to achieve your recovery goals. List them:

_____

_____

_____

You have used a two-part mapping process to separate the I-System's controlled action steps from the recovery action steps. You discovered that the items on your bridging awareness map that come without body tension and mind clutter are all recovery action steps that come from natural functioning. Choose the recovery action step that is the most important to you and put it into action today. For success in achieving your recovery goals, you need to do each action step with a quiet I-System. If you have body tension and mind clutter come up when you are doing your action steps, use your recovery tools to quiet your I-System. With the I-System no longer in charge, your choices now come from your natural functioning, and the recovery action steps are done by your true self.

PUT YOUR TRUE SELF IN CHARGE OF YOUR RECOVERY PROGRAM

1. As you experienced in the previous exercise, any recovery activity or practice can either be driven by the I-System's damaged self or by the natural functioning of your true self. In the next map, write down one of your recovery program activities or practices (for example, *Going to meetings, Meditating daily, Jogging three times a week*) in the oval below. Next, take a couple of minutes to write around the oval your thoughts about this specific recovery activity or practice. Be specific. Describe your body tension at the bottom of the map.

RECOVERY PROGRAM MAP

A. Is your I-System switch on or off? _____ If you are experiencing no body tension or mind clutter when doing this map, then your recovery practice is driven by the natural functioning of your true self. If your I-System switch is on, rate your I-System activity from 1 to 10 _____, and answer the questions below.

B. What are your depressors/fixers/storylines?

_____

_____

C. What are your requirements?

_____

If your map indicated an active I-System, then your recovery activity is I-System driven and has become a fixer activity.

180

2. Do this map again using bridging awareness practices. Write the same activity or practice in the oval. Before you start writing about your recovery activity or practice, listen to background sounds and feel your body's pressure on your seat, your feet on the floor, and the pen in your hand. Take your time. Once you are settled, keep feeling the pen in your hand as you start writing. Watch the ink go onto the paper, and keep listening to background sounds. Write for a couple of minutes.

RECOVERY PROGRAM MAP WITH BRIDGING

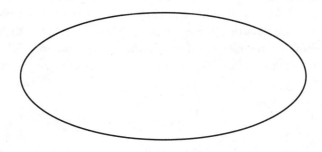

A. Is there a difference between this map and the first map?

_____

B. Is your I-System still active in this map? If so, do the map again and use your recovery tools to defuse the requirements you have until your recovery activity or practice is free from I-System activity and is now driven by the natural functioning of your true self.

_____

C. Repeat this two-part map exercise for each of your recovery program activities and practices until your true self is in charge of every aspect of your recovery program.

You have used a two-part mapping process to identify who has been in control of your recovery program—your I-System or your true self. You have put your naturally powerful true self back in charge. By continuing to use the recovery tools learned in this workbook to reduce the activity of your I-System, you will ensure that your true self remains in charge. When your recovery program is managed by natural functioning, it's not driven by a futile attempt to fix that which is not broken. The recovery of your true self in each and every moment has been long overdue. Being connected to your source of goodness, healing, and wisdom, right here and right now is all it takes.

REVIEW

Discover

- How the I-System corrupts your recovery.

- The difference between a fixer-driven recovery goal and a natural functioning recovery goal.

- Your recovery action steps to achieve your recovery goals.

Experience

- You have experienced using all of your mind-body bridging recovery tools, and have mapped, recognized, and defused many of your requirements. These tools quiet your I-System so that you can manage any situation that comes up in your life. Remember, each moment that your I-System is in control is a moment filled with unnecessary suffering. When your true self, in a natural functioning state, is handling a situation, the choices you make guide you to your best life.

Apply

- Make a habit of using your recovery tools to reduce the activity of your I-System in your daily life, and do at least one map a day.

- Use your body as a compass by noticing your personal and unique signs of body tension (stomach tight, shaky hands) that always come before you enter into an addicted mode. Then use all of your recovery tools to move into natural functioning.

- Use power mapping when you have stubbornly hidden requirements that create body tension and mental distress.

- Live a full life with an I-System at rest.

Recovery tools

➢ Use power mapping to map your way out of difficult-to-defuse requirements.

➢ Defuse requirements to manage your urges and cravings.

➢ Use recovery action steps for healthy recovery choices.

MBB RATING SCALE: ACHIEVE LASTING RECOVERY AND LIVE YOUR BEST LIFE

Date: _____

After using the tools in this chapter for several days, check the description that best matches your practice: hardly ever, sometimes, usually, or almost always.

How often do you...	Hardly Ever	Sometimes	Usually	Almost Always
Listen to background sounds?				
Sense the sensation under your fingers when you take a drink?				
Experience gravity?				
Use bridging practices to reduce anxiety symptoms?				
Become really aware of your daily activities, like making the bed, eating, and driving?				
Hear the water going down the drain and experience the water on your body when you are showering or washing your hands?				
Use bridging to help you sleep?				
Use bridging to help you relax and stay focused?				
Notice body sensations as a sign of an active I-System?				
Realize that an active I-System is underlying your anxiety?				
Notice your depressor?				
Notice your fixer?				
Defuse your depressor?				
Defuse your fixer?				
Recognize storylines?				
Realize that requirements are causing your daily upsets?				
Recognize and defuse your requirements?				

Notice when the damaged self is in charge?				
Realize that the damaged self is a myth of the I-System?				
Recognize when you are in the executive mode?				
Notice when your true self is functioning moment by moment?				
Make daily mind-body maps?				
Use power mapping?				
Use your anxiety reduction tools?				
Live life in the executive mode, with your powerful self in charge?				

MBB QUALITY OF LIFE GAUGE

Date: _____

Only do this gauge when you have made a habit of using the anxiety reduction tools from this workbook in your life. Compare your scores with those from the quality of life gauges in chapters 1 and 4. This gauge lets you measure your progress and keep track of your life-changing experience.

Over the past seven days, how did you do in these areas?

Circle the number under your answer.	Not at all	Several days	More than half the days	Nearly every day
1. I've had positive interest and pleasure in my activities.	0	1	3	5
2. I've felt optimistic, excited, and hopeful.	0	1	3	5
3. I've slept well and woken up feeling refreshed.	0	1	3	5
4. I've had lots of energy.	0	1	3	5
5. I've been able to focus on tasks and use self-discipline.	0	1	3	5
6. I've stayed healthy, eaten well, exercised, and had fun.	0	1	3	5
7. I've felt good about my relationships with my family and friends.	0	1	3	5
8. I've been satisfied with my accomplishments at home, work, or school.	0	1	3	5
9. I've been comfortable with my financial situation.	0	1	3	5
10. I've felt good about the spiritual base of my life.	0	1	3	5
11. I've been satisfied with the direction of my life.	0	1	3	5
12. I've felt fulfilled, with a sense of well-being and peace of mind.	0	1	3	5

Score Key: Column Total   ____   ____   ____   ____

0–15 . . . . Poor

16–30 . . . . Fair   Total Score _____

31–45 . . . . Good

46 and above . . . . Excellent

CONCLUSION

By finishing this workbook you have gained skills to allow you to live your life in natural functioning with an I-System at rest. By utilizing the recovery tools you have learned in this workbook, you can now live your best recovery lifestyle with your true self in charge.

After completing this workbook, Libby shared with us how she is now taking control of her life. She was having problems in her relationship with her boyfriend. She decided to do a two-part map about her tumultuous relationship with Todd. She clearly saw her depressors (*I'm unlovable, I'm not good enough for him*), her fixers (*Work hard to make Todd love me; Use drugs*), and her endless storylines about whose fault it was that the relationship was not working. She saw her requirements (*Todd should love me, I should please him, I should be lovable, I should be strong*). On her second map, her I-System rested and she was calm and relaxed. The only items were life can be better than this; I'm O.K. Once she completed her maps, she began to immediately utilize every bit of awareness and knowing in her life. When Todd called her that evening, Libby recognized her requirement (*Todd should really love me*). His tone of voice and self-preoccupation violated her requirement, but she smiled in relief that she had defused that requirement and was able to deal actively and assertively with this failing relationship.

Be like Libby and ask yourself after each two-part map you do, *How will my awareness and knowing on my maps help me reduce the activity of my I-System and allow me to live my best life here and now?*

The appendixes of this book contain a two-part mapping template for your daily ongoing mapping practice. Each two-part map you do puts troubling issues in front of you. The first map lets you see how your active I-System works to keep your addicted mode going. The second map allows you to see your troubling issue from a position where you have access to your wellspring of healing, goodness, and wisdom. Awareness and knowing are not enough! To heal your addiction, you must close the awareness/knowing/doing loop by immediately carrying what you have gained from your maps into your life.

Recovery Tools

CHAPTER 1

> ➤ Recognize when your I-System is active (on) or inactive (off).

> ➤ Thought labeling

> ➤ Bridging awareness practices:

  • Awareness of background sounds

  • Awareness of what you are touching

  • Awareness of colors, facial features, and shapes

  • Awareness of your body sensations

CHAPTER 2

> ➤ Create two-part mind-body maps whenever you begin to feel yourself moving into an addicted mode. A map a day helps to keep the cravings at bay.

> ➤ Discover how requirements activate your I-System.

➤ Recognize requirements to quiet your I-System.

➤ Use your body as a compass by befriending your body.

CHAPTER 3

➤ Recognize the depressor's activity.

➤ Become aware of your storyline.

➤ Defuse the depressor.

CHAPTER 4

➤ Recognize the depressor/fixer cycle.

➤ Defuse the fixer.

➤ Convert fixer activity into natural functioning.

CHAPTER 5

➤ Defuse your requirements for yourself, others, and situations.

CHAPTER 6

➤ Defuse your requirements for yourself.

➤ Defuse your requirements for your relationships.

➤ Mirror mapping

CHAPTER 7

➤ Expand your awareness to recognize signs of emotions taken over by the I-System.

➤ Use non-judgmental awareness to calm your I-System and restore your natural emotions.

➤ Bubble map the troubling items (thoughts associated with excess body tension) when your requirements are unclear.

➤ Befriend your emotions.

CHAPTER 8

➤ Use power mapping to map your way out of difficult-to-defuse requirements.

➤ Defuse requirements to manage your urges and cravings.

➤ Use recovery action steps for healthy recovery choices.

MIND-BODY BRIDGING DAILY MAPPING GUIDE

1. Choose a mapping topic and write it in the oval. It may be as simple as "What's on My Mind?" or as specific as a certain troubling, addictive situation. Next, take a couple of minutes to write around the oval your thoughts about that topic. Be specific. Describe your body tension at the bottom of the map.

CHOOSE YOUR TOPIC MAP

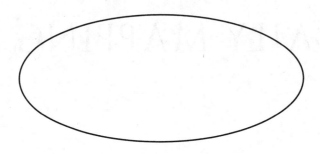

Body Tension: _____

A. Is your I-System on or off? _____   If it's on, rate your I-System activity from 1 to 10: _____

B. On your map place a "D" next to your depressor thoughts and an "F" next to the fixer thoughts.

C. List your storylines.

_____

_____

D. What are your requirements? List them:

_____

_____

E. How do you act in this mind-body state?

_____

2. Do this map again using bridging awareness practices. Write the same topic in the oval. Before you start writing about the topic, listen to background sounds and feel your body's pressure on your seat, your feet on the floor, and the pen in your hand. Take your time. Once you are settled, keep feeling the pen in your hand as you start writing. Watch the ink go onto the paper, and keep listening to background sounds. Write for a couple of minutes.

CHOOSE YOUR TOPIC MAP WITH BRIDGING

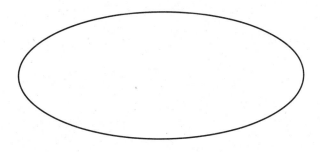

A. Is your I-System on or off? _____   If it's on, rate your I-System activity from 1 to 10: _____

B. How is this map the same as or different from the previous one?

_____

C. How do you act in this mind-body state?

_____

D. Are you able to defuse the requirement on the previous map?   Yes _____   No _____

E. What are you going to do with what you have learned from your two-part map?

_____

_____

F. How will it keep your damaged self out of the driver's seat today and tomorrow?

_____

APPENDIX B

MIND-BODY LANGUAGE

CHAPTER 1:

I-System: Each of us has an I-System, and it's either active (on) or resting (off). When it's on, it creates dysfunction in your mind-body. You know the I-System is on when your mind is cluttered with spinning thoughts, your body is tense, your awareness is contracted, and your mental and physical functioning is impaired. It's called the I-System because it prompts you to falsely identify with the spinning thoughts and the physical distress it causes.

Addicted mode: Addiction is best understood as a specific, habitual, and temporal way of existing, relating, and living, which is characterized by habitual substance abuse and loss of control.

True self: How you think, feel, see the world, and act when your I-System is resting. Your true self is always present in the natural functioning state, where your mind and body work in harmony, as a healing unit.

Damaged self: How you think, feel, see the world, and act when your I-System is active. Life is overwhelming, your natural functioning is impaired, and you struggle to control your addicted mode.

Mind-body bridging: When you use the tools in this workbook, you form a bridge from your damaged self with an active I-System to your true self in the natural functioning state, which handles daily life in a smooth and healthy way.

CHAPTER 2:

Requirements: Thoughts made into mental rules by your I-System that tell how you and the world should be in each moment. When your I-System rules are not met, you become filled with body tension and troubling thoughts. Unmet requirements will always put you in the addicted mode.

Recognize requirements: When you become clearly aware that your requirement—not the events around you—is making your I-System active, you curtail the activity of your I-System and begin self-healing in a natural functioning state.

CHAPTER 3:

Depressor: A part of the I-System that takes your natural negative thoughts and self-talk (things you say to yourself) and creates body tension and mind clutter. It constitutes a major part of your habitual addictive thinking patterns. It makes you feel weak, powerless, and vulnerable, and it fuels your addicted mode.

Storyline: Thoughts that your I-System spins into stories (true or not) that sustain your I-System and substance abuse, and pull you away from what you are presently doing.

Defusing the depressor: When you become clearly aware that your negative thoughts are "just thoughts," you reduce the power of the depressor. This allows your mind-body to start healing from your addiction.

CHAPTER 4:

Fixer: The depressor's partner that drives your substance abuse and daily activities with overactive, never-ending thoughts of how to fix yourself and the world.

Defusing the fixer: When you become clearly aware (at the time you are doing something) that your fixer is active and use your recovery tools, you take away the fixer's power. Right away, you feel a shift from a stressful, addicted mode to one with a ready and relaxed mind and body. You can now calmly take care of yourself and whatever you have to do in natural functioning.

Depressor/fixer cycle: These I-System partners create a vicious cycle, keeping the I-System going and sustaining your addiction.

CHAPTER 5:

Defusing requirements: When you use all your recovery tools, you handle a situation that used to cause you distress (turn on your I-System) with a ready and relaxed mind-body. Even when the I-System's picture of how you and the world should be is not fulfilled, the defused requirement is powerless to turn on your I-System and cause you to relapse.

CHAPTER 8:

Recovery action steps: Actions you take to achieve a recovery goal that come from the two-part mind-body mapping process, and are carried out by your naturally functioning true self.

REFERENCES

Alcoholics Anonymous World Services Inc. 1976. *Alcoholics Anonymous* (3rd Ed). New York: AA World Services.

Beck, J. S. 1995. *Cognitive Therapy: Basics and Beyond.* New York: Guilford Press.

Block, S. H., and C. B. Block. 2007. *Come to Your Senses: Demystifying the Mind-Body Connection.* 2nd ed. New York: Atria Books/Beyond Words Publishing.

Block, S. H., and C. B. Block. 2010. *Mind-Body Workbook for PTSD: A 10-Week Program for Healing After Trauma.* Oakland, CA: New Harbinger Publications.

Block, S. H., and C. B. Block. 2012. *Mind-Body Workbook for Stress: Effective Tools for Lifelong Stress Reduction and Crisis Management.* Oakland, CA: New Harbinger Publications.

Block, S. H., and C. B. Block. 2013. *Mind-Body Workbook for Anger: Effective Tools for Anger Management and Conflict Resolution.* Oakland, CA: New Harbinger Publications.

Block, S. H., and C. B. Block. 2014. *Mind-Body Workbook for Anxiety: Effective Tools for Overcoming Panic, Fear and Worry.* Oakland, CA: New Harbinger Publications.

Block, S. H., S. H. Ho, and Y. Nakamura. 2009. *A Brain Basis for Transforming Consciousness with Mind-Body Bridging.* Paper presented at Toward a Science of Consciousness Conference, June 12, at Hong Kong Polytechnical University, Hong Kong, China, Abstract 93.

Bowen, S., N. Chawla, and A. Marlatt. 2011. *Mindfulness-Based Relapse Prevention for Addictive Behaviours.* New York: Guilford Press.

Boly, M., C. Phillips, E. Balteau, C. Schnakers, C. Degueldre, G. Moonen, et al. 2008. Consciousness and Cerebral Baseline Activity Fluctuations. *Human Brain Mapping* 29 (7): 868–74.

Boly, M., C. Phillips, L. Tshibanda, A. Vanhaudenhuyse, M. Schabus, T. T. Dang-Vu, G. Moonen, R. Hustinx, P. Maquet, and S. Laureys. 2008. Intrinsic Brain Activity in Altered States of Consciousness: How Conscious Is the Default Mode of Brain Function? *Annals of the New York Academy of Sciences* 1129: 119–29.

Bradshaw, J. 1988. *Healing the Shame that Binds You*. Deerfield Beach, FL: Health Communications Inc.

Cole, M. W., J. R. Reynolds, J. D. Power, G. Repovs, A. Anticevic, and T. S. Braver. 2013. Multi-task Connectivity Reveals Flexible Hubs for Adaptive Task Control. *Nature Neuroscience* 16 (9): 1348–55.

Du Plessis, G. P. 2012. Toward an Integral Model of Addiction: By Means of Integral Methodological Pluralism as a Metatheoretical and Integrative Conceptual Framework. *Journal of Integral Theory and Practice* 7 (3): 1–24.

Du Plessis, G. P. 2015. *An Integral Guide to Recovery: Twelve Steps and Beyond*. Tucson, AZ: Integral Publishers.

Flores, P. J. 1997. *Group Psychotherapy with Addicted Populations*. Binghamton, NY: The Haworth Press Inc.

Lipschitz, D. L., R. Kuhn, A. Y. Kinney, G. W. Donaldson, and Y. Nakamura. 2013. Reduction in Salivary Alpha-Amylase Levels Following a Mind-Body Intervention in Cancer Survivors. *Psychoneuroendocrinology* 38 (9): 1521–31.

Lipschitz, D. L., R. Kuhn, A. Y. Kinney, K. Grewen, G. W. Donaldson, and Y. Nakamura. 2015. An Exploratory Study of the Effects of Mind-Body Interventions Targeting Sleep on Salivary Oxytocin Levels in Cancer Survivors. *Integrated Cancer Therapies* 14 (4): 366–80.

Marlatt, G. A., and J. R. Gordon. (Eds.). 1985. *Relapse Prevention: Maintenance Strategies in the Treatment of Addictive Behaviors* (1st ed.). New York: Guilford Press.

Narcotics Anonymous World Services, Inc. 1993. *It Works: How and Why*. Chatsworth, CA: Narcotics Anonymous World Services, Inc.

Nakamura, Y., D. L. Lipschitz, R. Kuhn, A. Y. Kinney, and G. W. Donaldson. 2013. Investigating Efficacy of Two Brief Mind-Body Intervention Programs for Managing Sleep Disturbance in Cancer Survivors: A Pilot Randomized Controlled Trial. *Journal of Cancer Survivorship* 7 (2): 165–82.

Nakamura, Y., D. L. Lipschitz, R. Landward, R. Kuhn, and G. West. 2011. Two Sessions of Sleep-Focused Mind-Body Bridging Improve Self-Reported Symptoms of Sleep and PTSD in Veterans: A Pilot Randomized Controlled Trial. *Journal of Psychosomatic Research* 70 (4): 335–45.

Nakamura, Y., D. L. Lipschitz, E. Kanarowski, T. McCormick, D. Sutherland, and M. Melow-Murchie. 2015. Investigating Impacts of Incorporating an Adjuvant Mind-Body Intervention Method Into Treatment as Usual at a Community-Based Substance Abuse Treatment Facility: A Pilot Randomized Controlled Study. *SAGE Open* 5 (1), 2158244015572489.

Tollefson, D. R., K. Webb, D. Shumway, S. H. Block, and Y. Nakamura. 2009. A Mind-Body Approach to Domestic Violence Perpetrator Treatment: Program Overview and Preliminary Outcomes. *Journal of Aggression, Maltreatment, and Trauma* 18 (1): 17–45.

Weissman, D. H., K. C. Roberts, K. M. Visscher, and M. G. Woldorff. 2006. The Neural Bases of Momentary Lapses in Attention. *Nature Neuroscience* 9 (7): 971–78.

ACKNOWLEDGMENTS

The addiction workbook has been developed with the help and feedback of individuals suffering from addiction. Over the past fifteen years they have shared with us how they used mind-body bridging to heal from their addiction. We are grateful for the enormous contribution of the 12-step programs and the pioneering work of others in the field of substance abuse recovery and relapse prevention. The clinicians from around the world using, developing, and refining mind-body bridging have our gratitude. Deserving of specific mention are the members of the International Mind-Body Bridging Board of Professional Standards: Don Glover, Rich Landward, Theresa McCormick, Andrea Phillips, Isaac Phillips, Kevin Webb, and Heli Jussila Martineau. The Mind-Body Bridging Certification Program at the College of Social Work at the University of Utah under the leadership of Dorann Mitchell is of great importance. The research efforts of Yoshi Nakamura, David Lipschitz, Derrik Tollefson, and Shaun Ho to establish a firm evidence basis for mind-body bridging are much appreciated. The support of the Integral recovery community was most welcome. Andrea A. Peters has ably assisted in the preparation of this workbook. The direction from the editors of New Harbinger Publications was most helpful.

Stanley H. Block, MD, is adjunct professor of psychiatry at the University of Utah School of Medicine, and a board-certified psychiatrist and psychoanalyst. He is a consultant on the medical staff at US Army and Veterans Administration Hospitals. He lectures and consults with treatment centers worldwide, and is coauthor of *Mind-Body Workbook for Stress*, *Mind-Body Workbook for PTSD*, *Mind-Body Workbook for Anger*, and *Come to Your Senses*. He and his wife, Carolyn Bryant Block, live in Copalis Beach, WA. Find out more about his work online at http://www.mindbodybridging.com.

Carolyn Bryant Block is coauthor of *Bridging the I-System*, *Come to Your Senses*, *Mind-Body Workbook for PTSD*, *Mind-Body Workbook for Stress*, and *Mind-Body Workbook for Anger*. She is codeveloper of mind-body bridging.

Guy du Plessis, MA, is a faculty mentor in the School of Behavioral Sciences at California Southern University, faculty member at the Wayne Institute for Advanced Psychotherapy at Bellarmine University, a board-certified counselor, and specializes in addiction treatment and research. Du Plessis has worked in the addiction treatment milieu for over fifteen years as a counselor, head of treatment, program and clinical director, and researcher. He is author of the book *An Integral Guide to Recovery*, developer of the Integrated Recovery Program, and has published numerous academic articles in the fields of addiction studies, theoretical psychology, and philosophy.

Rich Landward, LCSW, MPA, is assistant professor in the College of Social Work at the University of Utah. He specializes in using mind-body bridging to treat post-traumatic stress, anxiety, and substance use in children, adolescents, and adults.

Foreword writer **Robert Weathers, PhD**, holds a PhD in clinical psychology, and is currently the full-time academic effectiveness coordinator at California Southern University. His recent university work includes developing curriculum in their new, nationally approved Addiction Studies Certificate program, as well as mindfulness-based, graduate-level clinical training coursework.

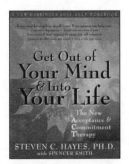

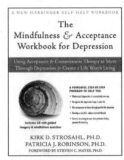

FROM OUR PUBLISHER—

As the publisher at New Harbinger and a clinical psychologist since 1978, I know that emotional problems are best helped with evidence-based therapies. These are the treatments derived from scientific research (randomized controlled trials) that show what works. Whether these treatments are delivered by trained clinicians or found in a self-help book, they are designed to provide you with proven strategies to overcome your problem.

Therapies that aren't evidence-based—whether offered by clinicians or in books—are much less likely to help. In fact, therapies that aren't guided by science may not help you at all. That's why this New Harbinger book is based on scientific evidence that the treatment can relieve emotional pain.

This is important: if this book isn't enough, and you need the help of a skilled therapist, use the following resources to find a clinician trained in the evidence-based protocols appropriate for your problem. And if you need more support—a community that understands what you're going through and can show you ways to cope—resources for that are provided below, as well.

Real help is available for the problems you have been struggling with. The skills you can learn from evidence-based therapies will change your life.

Matthew McKay, PhD
Publisher, New Harbinger Publications

**If you need a therapist, the following organization
can help you find a therapist trained in cognitive behavioral therapy (CBT).**

The Association for Behavioral & Cognitive Therapies (ABCT) Find-a-Therapist service offers a list of therapists schooled in CBT techniques. Therapists listed are licensed professionals who have met the membership requirements of ABCT and who have chosen to appear in the directory.
Please visit www.abct.org and click on *Find a Therapist*.

**For additional support for patients, family, and friends,
please contact the following:**

Anxiety and Depression Association of American (ADAA) **www.adaa.org**

Depression and Bipolar Support Alliance (DBSA) **www.dbsalliance.org**

National Suicide Prevention Lifeline
Call 24 hours a day 1-800-273-TALK (8255) or visit www.suicidepreventionlifeline.org